DO I NEED A WILL OR A TRUST?

WILL

TRUST

By

Taylor Phillip Willingham, J.D. M.S.

Estate Planning College
7701 Eldorado Pkwy Ste. 200,
McKinney, Texas 75070
Printed in the United States of America

Second Edition

TABLE OF CONTENTS

Acknowledgement 6

Introduction: The Answer 7

PART 1 ESTATE PLANNING 15

1: Why We Plan For The Future 17

2: Failing to Plan 23

3: Inter Vivos Gifts 33

4. Social Media Planning 39

PART 2: WILLS & TRUSTS 49

5. History of Wills.. 51

6: Will Formalities 57

7. History of Trusts 63

8: Trust Purpose 72

9: Avoid Probate Without a Trust 81

PART 3: REASONS TO CREATE A TRUST 97

10: Blended Family Nightmare.. 99

11: Protecting Minor Children 109

12: Probate Avoidance 119

13: Creditor Protection Trusts.. 125

15: Beneficiary Protection 149

16: Protect Your Privacy.. 159

17: Multi-Generational Planning 165

18: Professional Management... 173

19: Safeguarding Against Your Future Self......................... 180

20: Appoint Your Own Judge 186

21: Qualified Income Trusts and Irrevocable Trust for Long-Term Care......193

22: Epilogue: After Getting a Living Trust..198

DISCLAIMER:

Taylor Willingham is an attorney based in Texas, and the insights within this book are grounded in Texas law. It is important to recognize that this book should not serve as the only reference for legal matters related to estate planning. For advice tailored to your specific situation, it is essential to consult with an attorney licensed in your jurisdiction.

Acknowledgement

Thank you to the numerous clients who have shared their feedback with me. Their invaluable insights, particularly regarding the confusion between wills and trusts, were instrumental in the creation of this book. Without their candid perspectives, this endeavor might not have come to fruition.

Special appreciation goes to Ben Russell and Kari Reddick for their diligent editing efforts. Their commitment to refining my grammar and clarifying complex legal concepts for the lay reader has been essential to this project.

I extend my deepest gratitude to my wife for her unwavering support, especially during the countless evenings dedicated to writing this book a second time. Additionally, I am immensely grateful to my team for their extra efforts and support, which allowed me the time and space to focus on this significant work.

Introduction: The Answer

Marcus Aurelius Antoninus governed the Roman Empire from 161 to 180 CE. Described as "the noblest of all the men who, by sheer intelligence and force of character, have prized and achieved goodness for its own sake and not for any reward," [1] he exemplified unwavering character and determination throughout his 19-year reign. Not only was he a remarkable leader, but he was also recognized as a disciplined stoic philosopher and a genius. Reflecting on Marcus' consistent character from his youth to his role as Emperor of Rome, Cassias Dio observed, "he remained the same and did not change in the least." [2]

---

[1] Grant, M. *The Climax of Rome.* (Weidenfeld, 1993) p. 139.

[2] Dio lxxii. 36, 72.34

Marcus Aurelius was part of a lineage known as the "Five Good Emperors," which included Nerva, Trajan, Hadrian, Antoninus Pius, and himself. This era was marked by a unique succession practice: each emperor, except for Marcus, was chosen for their merit and adopted by the preceding emperor, not by blood relation. This system fostered a period of prosperity and stability in the Roman Empire, as each emperor was selected based on capability and virtue.

However, Marcus Aurelius diverged from this successful model of adoption when he appointed his biological son, Commodus, as his successor. Commodus became co-emperor in 177 CE and fully succeeded his father in 180 CE. This decision contrasted sharply with the philosophies and governance styles of the Five Good Emperors. A stark departure from Marcus' stoic principles of self-restraint, duty, and respect for others was noted by an author: "Marcus' legacy is tragic, because the emperor's stoic philosophy…was so abjectly abandoned by the imperial line he anointed on his death." [3] Commodus' reign, unlike his predecessors, was disastrous and marked a significant decline from the standards set by the Five Good Emperors, ultimately impacting the Roman Empire adversely.

Throughout the extensive history of the Roman Empire, records indicate that there were more than 197 emperors. Among these, five emperors are distinguished as exceptional leaders, notably for their selection based on merit rather than lineage. The instinct to secure one's legacy for future generations is a common one. However, entrusting an empire to an ill-suited heir can lead to catastrophic outcomes. This book will explore how the legal

---

[3] 'THINKERS AT WAR' – Marcus Aurelius'. *Military History Monthly*, published 2014.

framework of trusts was developed to address this precise challenge, offering a way to extend the benefits of one's legacy to their descendants while ensuring competent management.

Fortunately, the repercussions of inadequate future planning in our lives are not as dire as those faced by Roman emperors, where neglect could trigger widespread misery or even herald a descent into the Dark Ages. However, the consequences for our loved ones and those under our care can still be significant. Consider a client of mine who built a thriving business employing over 50 people. He intended for his son to take over upon reaching maturity. While my client was extraordinary, the likelihood of his son maintaining the success of such a large enterprise was slim. He was on the verge of repeating the same mistake Marcus Aurelius made nearly 2,000 years ago, bequeathing his empire to his eldest son. That changed when he became acquainted with the concept of a trust.

Through my experience in probating over a thousand cases, the contrast between those who have prepared for the future and those who have not is striking. Although the law provides certain safeguards to lessen the impact of dying intestate (without a will), these provisions often fall short. You possess the ability to far exceed these basic legal protections, greatly enhancing the welfare of your closest relatives and associates.

Wills and Trusts: Distinctly Different Entities

It's a common misconception that wills and trusts are similar, likely due to years of attorneys marketing them together. However, it's crucial to understand that they are fundamentally different legal tools. Think of them as entirely separate entities in your mind, breaking away from the idea that they are alike. This confusion is often exacerbated in seminars where the legal distinctions between a will and a trust aren't adequately explained.

A will is a legal document that only takes effect upon death. Its primary functions are (1) to transfer property and (2) to nominate an executor. While it is sometimes referred to as a "death deed," this term can be misleading as many are unfamiliar with what a deed actually entails. Although a will has capabilities beyond these two functions, let's focus on its essential elements for simplicity.

A trust is a legal arrangement separating legal and equitable property titles. Don't be daunted by the legal jargon; this concept is more familiar than it seems. Consider the example of renting a property. While renting doesn't establish a trust, it does split property interest. As a tenant, you have the right to occupy the property, whereas the landlord retains the right to receive rents. Property rights are similarly divided in a trust: (1) the right to manage the property and (2) the right to benefit from the property.

Understanding this, it becomes clear that wills and trusts are entirely different. They intersect when a trust is created to manage property after someone's death, which is a primary source of confusion. In such scenarios, a person might assign the legal interest (management of the property) to one individual and the beneficial interest (enjoyment of the property) to another. We will delve deeper into this topic later, clarifying the unique roles and functions of wills and trusts in estate planning.

The Answer: Deciphering Wills and Trusts

While reading this book might not top your list of enjoyable activities, I urge you to consider this concise overview before proceeding. A frequent question I encounter is, "Do I need a will or a trust?" Sometimes, rephrasing a question is as enlightening as answering it. The more pertinent inquiry is, "Do I need a trust?" The need for a will is universal; there are no exceptions. In fact, during the 12th and 13th centuries, the Catholic Church even viewed the absence of a will as sinful. This might be worth remembering before postponing your estate planning.

When contemplating whether to create a trust, consider these benefits:

1. **Managing a Blended Family Situation**: Blended families often face estate planning conflicts. Children from a previous marriage might feel sidelined by a newer spouse, leading to potential disputes and litigation. Trusts provide an effective way to safeguard the interests of both your spouse and children, ensuring your estate is distributed as you wish (Chapter 8).

2. **Protecting Minor Children**: Ensuring the well-being of your children in the event of your untimely demise is crucial (Chapter 9).

3. **Avoiding Probate**: Many seek trusts primarily to bypass probate. However, trusts must be properly funded to be effective in this regard, and there are alternative estate structuring methods to avoid probate (Chapter 10).

4. **Creditor Protection**: Using trusts for asset protection against creditors involves navigating various state laws. Trusts are more commonly used to safeguard your estate from your creditors (Chapter 11).

5. **Advanced Tax Planning**: Trusts can facilitate income-shifting strategies for high-net-worth individuals, potentially reducing tax liabilities (Chapter 12).

6. **Protecting Beneficiaries from Themselves**: A trust can restrict their access to funds if a beneficiary struggles with addiction or financial irresponsibility. It's also beneficial for disabled beneficiaries to supplement their government assistance (Chapter 13).

7. **Privacy Protection**: For those who value privacy or for public figures who wish to keep their assets confidential, trusts offer a solution (Chapter 14).

8. **Multi-Generational Benefits**: Trusts can ensure that funds intended for specific purposes, like a grandchild's education, are used as intended (Chapter 15).

9. **Professional Asset Management**: Trusts allow you to designate who will manage your estate, whether it be a family member or a financial institution (Chapter 16).

10. **Protection from Aging**: As mental faculties diminish with age, a trust can safeguard your estate from potential mismanagement (Chapter 17).

11. **Appointing a Trust Protector**: Trusts enable you to appoint someone to oversee and correct issues, minimizing legal disputes (Chapter 18).

12. **Safeguarding a Small Business**. Similar to the governance of the five good emperors, a trustee can hold legal title to oversee a business empire, ensuring its benefits are passed on to your heirs.

Addressing the Cost Concerns of Trusts

The cost factor is a pivotal consideration in estate planning, often influencing the decision of whether to create a trust. During consultations, I assess each client's unique situation to determine if a trust is genuinely necessary. However, my experience is that, more often than not, failure to create a trust is significantly more expensive in the long term.

I have a trust, and so do all my colleagues in estate planning. I even arranged a trust for my parents in Texas and advised my out-of-state family members to seek legal assistance for setting up their own. However, the urgency to invest in a trust isn't always immediate. I remember delaying forming my trust until a couple of years into my practice. The importance hit home when I encountered a young woman about my age seeking to probate her late husband's estate. Witnessing her situation made me realize the criticality of having a trust in place, prompting me to start the process for my own trust the following day.

It's crucial to weigh the costs against the benefits and future security that a trust can provide. The decision to invest in a trust should be based on a comprehensive evaluation of your financial situation and estate planning objectives. While a trust may not be immediately necessary for everyone, it can offer peace of mind and long-term benefits that justify the investment for many.

Clarifying Service Costs and Trust Decision-Making

Cost of Professional Services During 10 Years

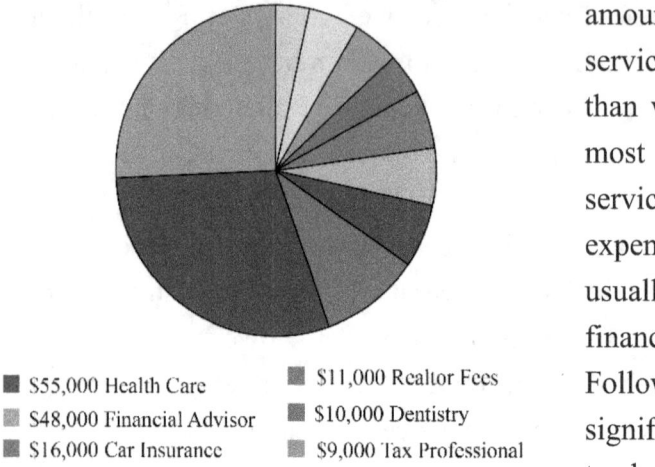

- ■ $55,000 Health Care
- ■ $48,000 Financial Advisor
- ■ $16,000 Car Insurance
- ■ $14,000 Home Services
- ■ $12,000 Life Insurance
- ■ $11,000 Realtor Fees
- ■ $10,000 Dentistry
- ■ $9,000 Tax Professional
- □ $7,000 Internet Services
- ■ $5,500 Attorney Services

Throughout your life, the amount spent on legal services is typically less than what you'll spend on most other professional services. The two biggest expenses in this regard are usually healthcare and financial planning. Following these, the next significant expenditure tends to be on insurance-based services. To give you a clearer perspective, consider the accompanying chart in the book, which illustrates the comparative costs of various services over a decade.

With this foundational knowledge, you're now equipped to make an informed decision about whether creating a trust is right for you. The rest of this book delves into detailed information and real-life scenarios to aid your understanding of trusts and their practical implications. It's beneficial to comprehend the nuances of how trusts function, but if certain aspects are more relevant to your situation, feel free to focus on those specific chapters. This approach will allow you to tailor your learning to your personal needs and circumstances, ensuring you have the most pertinent information to guide your decision on trust creation.

PART 1

ESTATE

PLANNING

1: Why We Plan For The Future

My inaugural publication, Why Should I Care, I'll be Dead, tackles a common quandary faced by my clients upon their initial consultation: the seeming futility of estate planning. Spanning 150 pages, this work advocates estate planning as pivotal to societal and familial continuity. It posits that the fabric of society is woven not by monumental acts by a select few but by the cumulative prudent decisions of its citizenry to prepare for the future.

Instead of delving into my book, a viewing of the Netflix series *After Life* may offer a deeper comprehension of the imperatives of planning for a better future. Set in the fictional Tambury, it chronicles Tony Johnson, a bereaved newspaper writer, who, instead of succumbing to his suicidal grief, adopts a reckless demeanor, believing in his impunity as a superpower. This facade gradually crumbles as Tony discovers that genuine fulfillment of life stems from altruism and connectivity. A pivotal moment mirrors the ethos of my book through Anne, a widow, who shares with Tony an ancient Greek proverb: "*A society grows great when old men plant trees in whose shade they know they shall never sit.*"

I am particularly fond of the Well Digger's tale, a true testament to foresight and planning for the future.

In a bygone era, a chieftain and his tribe were relegated to a desolate desert, having been ousted from every fertile territory they attempted to inhabit. Despite the despair this choice caused among his kin, the chieftain was steadfast in his determination to forge a brighter tomorrow. His resolve led to two monumental achievements: securing a crucial water supply for his tribe and establishing sovereignty over the land.

As time passed, his endeavors began to bear fruit, turning the barren desert into a thriving oasis. Yet, this newfound prosperity did not come without its challenges. A neighboring tribe, green with envy, forcibly took control of one of the chieftain's key wells. Known as the Well Digger, the chieftain opted for diplomacy over warfare, proposing to purchase the well back rather than engage in conflict.

This act of humility and foresight prompted the rival leader to cease hostilities and agree to a truce. Nevertheless, wary of the peace's durability, the Well Digger planted a grove of trees as a safeguard, ensuring a legacy of tranquility for his people. The descendants of the Well Digger continue to enjoy the shade provided by these trees, located near the storied site of Abraham's Well.

Abraham's legacy offers us a profound, intangible inheritance that continues to enrich our lives. The foundational spirit of this remarkable figure has been a source of inspiration for three of the world's major religions, each striving to embody his exemplary virtues and teachings. The moral here is profound: prudent individuals lay foundations from which their future generations will benefit. I invite you to embark on this journey with me, to establish legacies for your loved ones and contribute to the fabric of the society our forebears helped to shape.

Intangible Estate Planning

The most invaluable gift I've ever received was my father's journal. Amidst a challenging period, having emerged from law school and a master's program in Financial Planning with $150,000 in debt and facing limited job opportunities—the most promising of which offered a modest $36,000 annual salary—I found myself in dire financial straits. With the anticipation of a third child, I made the leap to establish my own law firm. This decision led me down the precarious path of relying on credit cards to fund the venture, a choice with predictably fraught consequences.

Bankruptcy loomed ominously on the horizon, challenging the very foundations of my faith—my belief in my career, my future, my family, and my spiritual convictions. These aspects had always formed the essence of my identity and my understanding of the world. Amidst this turmoil, I found myself losing grip on what I valued most, despite laboring through 14 to 15-hour days. My wife, my steadfast partner, shared this journey with me, her own apprehension mirroring mine. It was during this period of profound uncertainty that I turned to my father's journal, a cherished family heirloom that would ultimately anchor me and offer a path to reclaiming my sense of self.

Here's a brief overview of my family's background: At the tender age of three, my mother, grappling with mental and emotional health challenges, made the heart-wrenching decision to entrust our care to my father.

Recognizing her limitations, she chose what she believed was best for us under the circumstances. The adjustment period was incredibly tough, compounded by our precarious financial situation—we faced not only the loss of our mother but also our home. My father, working as a special education teacher, did everything within his power to support us. In an effort to find stability, he moved us from Utah to Texas for the summer, where we lived in a trailer on a piece of land owned by my grandfather. Despite the modest accommodations, including limited air conditioning and a small black and white TV, my father's resilience and positive outlook on life instilled in us a sense of contentment and happiness.

Eventually my father found us an apartment back in Utah. All of us kids slept in one room while my father took the living room couch. During this time, he amazingly worked as a teacher, served as an active church member, attended army reserve drills, and took classes for his master's degree. As my dad explains in his journal, *there must have been angels helping every step of the way...*

To add yet another layer of complication, my father called upon to go to Korea for a two-week long drill. Having no other option, he hired people in an adjacent apartment to watch over us while he was gone. Unfortunately, yet again a series of disastrous circumstances ensued, ending with my siblings and me being mercifully taken in by my sister's first-grade teacher in order to escape the abusive figure our caretaker turned out to be.

Upon returning from Korea, my father, truly anguished by the events, packed us up for the summer and we returned to the camper in Texas. It is at this point in the story that my father's journal—his legacy to me—truly came to bear upon my own life circumstances. He writes, *"I remember sitting at the table in the trailer wondering if I had done anything correct in my life. As usual, I started making a list. I have lost the list, but I remember the first thing I wrote--I got my Eagle. I dug my way out of feeling sorry for myself..."*

I cried. Sitting there that night mired in the mud slide that was my own life, reading about my father's life which contrastingly seemed an outright avalanche, I wept at his words. Particularly, where he wonders if he'd done anything right to that point—because that's precisely how I felt. My father could've just thrown up his hands in surrender; he could've left and given up his kids to the care of their grandparents, but he didn't. That was his crossroads and he emerged stronger, wiser and would go on to live a good life, for which to this day I am so very grateful. The poem of William Knox seemed so fitting for my situation, "For we are the same our fathers have been, we see the same sights that our fathers have seen; we drink the same stream, and view the same sun, and run the same course our fathers have run."

I was subsequently at my own crossroads, and my dad's journal became my scripture that night. I would work to scrap my way back into the fight, so to speak. And with his inspiration, I did just that. I realized later that the greatest gift my father ever gave me was not money, but the decision he made not to give up. A legacy of endurance was worth more than all the treasures of the world.

Okay, you're asking yourself right about now, *great story, but what exactly does this have to do with estate planning?* Those individuals who come to my office really prepared for estate planning do it for the people they love, not the assets they have accumulated. ***Imbedded deep within their souls is a desire to preserve, memorialize, and extend those relationships they have developed throughout their lifetimes***.

At its core, estate planning embodies the selfless act of planting trees under whose shade we may never sit and digging wells whose waters we may never taste, thereby providing our societies, communities, and families with the essential foundations to thrive and succeed.

2: Failing to Plan

The absence of a well-considered plan can inadvertently place our legacies in the hands of those ill-suited to honor them. This lesson is vividly illustrated in the tale of the Assyrian king, Sennacherib, who lived around 700 BCE. Understanding the importance of a succession plan for his empire and family, Sennacherib crafted a will to safeguard assets for his favored son, Esarhaddon, bypassing the then-presumptive heir. This will included the bequeathal of "certain bracelets, coronets, and other precious objects of gold, ivory, and precious stones" stored for safety in the temple of Nebo.

Upon the death of his eldest son, Ashur-Nadin-Shumi, in 694 BCE, Sennacherib faced a quandary. His second eldest, Arda-Mulissu, lacked the competence to govern the empire effectively. Consequently, Sennacherib revised his will a decade later, designating Esarhaddon as his successor and excluding Arda-Mulissu. This decision led to tragic consequences: Arda-Mulissu and another brother, Nabu-Shar-Usur, assassinated their father in

23

retaliation for this perceived slight. However, Sennacherib's foresight in selecting a capable successor proved judicious. Esarhaddon ascended to become a distinguished leader of the Assyrian empire, achieving notable victories such as the conquest of Egypt and the restoration of Babylon. Had Sennacherib failed to act, his empire and descendants would likely have endured the tumultuous and potentially disastrous reign of Arda-Mulissu.

Sennacherib's story underscores a crucial aspect of planning: the necessity of ongoing revision. Estate planning is not a one-time task but a dynamic process that should evolve with circumstances. Initial choices for executors or beneficiaries may require reevaluation as situations and relationships change. Adapting estate planning documents to reflect current realities ensures that our legacies are preserved and passed on in accordance with our true intentions.

Why Many Fail to Do Estate Planning

"Death, as the Psalmist says, is inevitable for everyone." [4] This certainty is accompanied by a significant likelihood, with a 50% chance of experiencing physical or mental disability for at least 90 days before death. Estate planning is unique in its universal applicability, yet many fail to engage in this critical process due to various reasons:

1. Unawareness of its importance,
2. Apathy towards planning,
3. Concerns about cost,

---

[4] William Shakespeare, King Henry, IV, Part II, Act III, Scene ii, 11. 35-36, in the Arden Edition of the Works of William Shakespeare, The Second Part of King Henry IV 97 (A. Humphreys 1996) (stated by Justice Robert Shallow).

4. The time and effort required,
5. The perceived complexity of the process,
6. A belief in insufficient assets to warrant planning,
7. Hesitation to confront one's own mortality.

Unknown Heirs

"Mr. Willingham, are we ready to proceed?" Judge Copeland inquired, glancing at the clock and noting the five-minute delay in starting.

"I am prepared, Your Honor. However, I've been unable to reach the attorney ad litem this morning," I responded, quickly verifying that my staff had sent out the required notice.

"Could you provide Ms. Anderson's contact information?" I handed over the ad litem's number to Judge Copeland. After a brief call with her office, he was connected to her cell phone.

The phone rang, and the ad litem answered, "Ms. Anderson, this is Judge Weldon Copeland from the Collin County Probate Court. Is this a good time?"

"Yes, Your Honor. My apologies for the delay. I'm en route, but there's new information relevant to this case," she replied. As an attorney, such updates are often concerning.

"Let's proceed over the phone to expedite matters," Judge Copeland suggested, giving me an apprehensive look.

Ms. Anderson revealed to the judge that the decedent, my client Beth's late husband, had fathered a child at age 14 who was subsequently adopted. Beth was astounded, having never known about this child. This information came from the decedent's older sister. We agreed to delay the hearing until Ms. Anderson could arrive in person.

Upon her arrival, Ms. Anderson presented evidence that the decedent was the presumed father of a 62-year-old woman in California. Beth was stunned, learning her husband of 55 years had a previously unmentioned child. The court determined that he had fathered two children, dividing his community property equally between them. Beth received a life estate in their homestead and a third of his separate real property.

Beth was distressed by the significant loss in her husband's estate, a consequence of inadequate estate planning. When someone passes away, they can be deemed intestate for two reasons: (1) failure to create a valid will, or (2) creating a will that fails to cover all property. Intestacy laws, varying by state, are the default rules governing property distribution after death. Moving between states can significantly alter how an estate is distributed.

During the peak of the Covid pandemic, a nurse visited our office seeking assistance. The doctor who owned the practice she worked at had recently passed away, and there was an urgent need to manage payroll. I advised her to identify a family member of the deceased. She eventually found his brother, and together, we facilitated the temporary emergency appointment of an administrator for the estate. Unfortunately, by the time all necessary arrangements were in place, the value of the practice, once worth millions, had significantly diminished to a fraction of its original worth.

The wife of a colleague, who was an estate planning attorney himself, reached out to me after her husband unexpectedly passed away without having properly arranged his own estate. This oversight required us to navigate the probate process to grant her control over his law firm. Collaborating with other attorneys, we managed to address his pending caseload effectively.

However, during the course of these events, his wife was taken aback by a startling discovery: the majority of his property was legally inherited by his children. This outcome was likely due to the default rules of intestacy, as there was no clear estate plan in place. This situation emphasized the critical need for thorough estate planning, a necessity that holds true even for experts in the field. It also brought to light the fact that, regardless of one's knowledge or expertise, successfully executing a comprehensive estate plan can be a challenging task.

The Perils of Neglecting Estate Planning

Failing to undertake proper estate planning can lead to catastrophic outcomes, not just for individuals and their immediate families, but also for entire empires and the course of history. This is exemplified by imagining a scenario where Sennacherib, the Assyrian king, neglects estate planning, resulting in his empire potentially falling into the hands of his least competent heir. Such a lack of foresight can dismantle a legacy that took lifetimes to build, leading to unnecessary conflict, financial ruin, and the loss of control over how one's assets are distributed.

Conversely, the intentional choice of a successor can mark the beginning of a golden age. This is illustrated by Nerva's selection of Trajan as his successor, which was not a decision born out of familial obligation but of strategic foresight and wisdom. Nerva's choice set the Roman Empire on a path to its greatest era, highlighting the transformative power of thoughtful succession planning.

Estate planning is not merely about distributing assets after one's death; it's about actively shaping the future, ensuring that one's legacy is managed according to their wishes and that their beneficiaries are protected and provided for. It underscores the importance of deliberate decision-making in legacy planning and the potential consequences of inaction.

Act and Save

In the midst of excruciating pain, my client displayed unwavering determination to secure his family's future. His dedication was not just in spirit; it manifested in the painstaking process of finalizing his estate plan, a testament to his love and foresight. Among the myriad tasks was a critical review of his life insurance policy, a safety net for his family, revealing a pivotal condition: the policy's validity hinged on his employment status.

Faced with a grim prognosis, he had exhausted all available leave, and his employer, aware of his deteriorating health, seemed eager to sever ties. This would normally lead to the cancellation of his $450,000 life insurance benefit, a scenario all too common yet obscure to many, who remain unaware that their workplace life insurance might be contingent on their employment.

Undeterred, he chose to continue working. Over the ensuing months, his workplace transformed in a way few ever witness. His colleagues rallied around him, crafting a makeshift bed at the office and assuming his responsibilities, a profound act of solidarity and compassion. His perseverance was not just for his own dignity but fueled by the intent to keep his life insurance policy active, ensuring his family's financial security.

His meticulous attention to his estate plan, under such harrowing circumstances, was a final act of love and protection. It was a battle fought not against his illness, but against the risk of leaving his family vulnerable. In his final weeks, the collective efforts of his coworkers and his own indomitable will ensured that his life insurance benefits remained intact, providing his wife and children with a significant financial cushion due to the loss of his income.

The True Value of an Estate Planning Attorney

Engaging an estate planning attorney extends far beyond the mere drafting of documents. It encompasses a comprehensive assurance that your estate plan is executed precisely as intended. This level of precision and reliability cannot be matched by online drafting tools, which, while convenient, lack the safeguard of professional accountability.

Consider the case of a client who worked as an underwriter for an insurance company. When discussing the costs of insuring her home, the annual premium was quoted at $5,940. This amount was allocated to protect her physical assets against unforeseen circumstances. However, when the conversation shifted towards safeguarding her estate—a collection of her life's work, aiming to ensure its proper transition to her children—the cost for my professional services amounted to $4,500. This comparison illuminated a crucial perspective: the investment in a professionally crafted estate plan is a relatively modest expense for the peace of mind and security it provides.

This analogy brings to light the essence of what an estate planning attorney offers: insurance. Not in the traditional sense of tangible assets, but insurance that your wishes will be honored, your legacy preserved, and your estate passed on to your heirs as seamlessly as possible. When you choose to work with an attorney, you're not just paying for documents; you're investing in a meticulous, personalized process that aligns with your unique circumstances and objectives. This professional guidance ensures that your estate planning is not only comprehensive but also complies with the latest legal standards, minimizing the risk of disputes or complications after your passing.

The value of this "insurance" cannot be overstated. It's a strategic investment in the future, ensuring that your estate planning is a durable, effective framework that accomplishes your goals and safeguards your loved ones' inheritance.

3: Inter Vivos Gifts

Alexander the Great amassed a fortune estimated at over 1.2 trillion dollars when adjusted for inflation, yet he is not deemed the wealthiest individual in history. The inevitability of time renders the vast accumulations of wealth insignificant, as both the richest and the poorest share the same fate in the end. Consider the example of the great Egyptian Sultan, Saladin. Known for his conquests across Syria, Arabia, Persia, Mesopotamia, and for reclaiming Jerusalem in 1187, Saladin recognized the fleeting nature of riches. He generously distributed his wealth during his lifetime, striving for peace in the regions he had subdued, and even compensated his defeated adversaries.

Saladin's legacy is also marked by his actions after death. In his will, he bequeathed his remaining wealth to religious figures of various faiths, requesting prayers for his soul. One of his final act was instructing his soldier to place a shroud on a spear and to say aloud on his death, "Behold all that remains of Emperor Saladin! Of all the states he had conquered; of all the provinces he had subdued; of the boundless treasures he had

33

amassed; of the countless wealth he possessed; he retained in dying, nothing but this shroud."

This historical context sets the stage for a crucial estate planning concept: inter vivos transfers, or the distribution of assets during one's lifetime. I often discuss this with clients, noting that it doesn't require waiting until one's demise to distribute wealth. This method reduces estate size, reduce taxes, allows the benefactor to witness the recipient's enjoyment, and aids in fulfilling charitable goals. Furthermore, it can simplify asset transfers outside of probate.

However, gifting property isn't always straightforward. Legal complexities often arise, necessitating the fulfillment of three critical criteria for a valid gift: a clear intention to give, the physical or constructive delivery of the gift, and the recipient's acceptance. These requirements are crucial, especially in complicated scenarios, such as when a donor reconsiders a gift, like an engagement ring post-breakup, or attempts to offload an undesirable asset to an unwilling recipient.

Giving While You're Living

In my consultation with Ishmael Khan about his estate planning, it became apparent that he didn't possess a substantial amount of property. This was surprising, given his background in medicine. As our conversation progressed, the reason for his relatively modest estate became clear. Ishmael had been exceedingly generous throughout his life, investing substantially in his family's future. He had financed the education of all his children and bought each of them a house to spare them the burden of mortgages. Additionally, he was funding his grandchildren's education.

Ishmael lived by a straightforward philosophy: he aimed to use his wealth to support his children during his lifetime, intending to die with little to his name. He preferred to witness the benefits of his children's inheritance firsthand. Remarkably, his children had become very successful and deeply cherished their father, with each offering him a home if he ever needed it. Consequently, Ishmael had little concern for his retirement needs.

After assessing Ishmael's situation, I concluded that a trust wasn't necessary for his estate plan. Instead, his plan included a Transfer on Death Deed, Wills, Financial Power of Attorney forms, HIPAA designation forms, Medical Power of Attorney forms, and Living Wills for himself and his spouse.

Ishmael's approach offers a valuable perspective on estate planning. By distributing assets during your lifetime, you have the opportunity to observe your beneficiaries' reactions. Mr. Khan shared his strategy with me, revealing that he used his generosity as a way to gauge his children's behavior. This allowed him to address any negative reactions while he was still alive, rather than leaving such matters in the hands of a trustee after his passing. Reflecting on your ultimate goals can guide your decision on whether to give now or later, and in Ishmael's case, his choice fostered both family success and mutual appreciation.

Beware of Fraudulent Transfers

My office frequently receives calls from individuals nearing the end of their life, wishing to transfer all their assets to loved ones in the form of an advancement, as previously defined. However, there's a common misconception that advancements can circumvent creditors, taxes, or

Medicaid liens. It's crucial to understand that a transfer made with such intentions can be considered a fraudulent transfer and does not legally avoid these obligations. Consulting with an attorney is the most prudent approach to discuss the appropriate methods for making an advancement, especially in situations involving creditors. Legal professionals are invaluable in guiding the transfer of assets from one generation to the next in a lawful and strategic manner.

Gifting or advancing property must be executed thoughtfully to maximize benefits for the family while avoiding legal pitfalls. Such strategies might negate the need for a will or trust, but they should always be undertaken with legal guidance. Transfers intended to defraud, including those aimed at circumventing government claims, can be criminally prosecutable.

A case in point involves Nick Johnson, who urgently needed a deed. His father, about to enter a nursing home, possessed only hunting land, a treasured family asset for generations. Nick's father wished for this land to be inherited by his children, not liquidated for his care costs. I advised Nick that the optimal solution was to transfer the property to his mother. Under Texas law, the community spouse (the non-institutionalized spouse) can be legally transferred all assets of the institutional spouse. We implemented an expanded spousal protected resource amount strategy to safeguard the land, ensuring its preservation within the family.

Tips and Tricks to Even Out an Inheritance

It's common for clients to express concerns about unequal financial support given to their children over the years. They often wish to rectify this perceived imbalance in their wills. However, I generally advise against this approach. My experience has shown that children, even those who received more during their parent's lifetime, can feel slighted if a will stipulates they receive a smaller share of the estate. Additionally, this strategy can be problematic because parents often use up most of their assets later in life, leaving less for the child who received less support previously.

My recommendation is to consider making gifts to your children while you are still alive, if feasible. If direct gifting isn't possible, another strategy is to allocate a larger portion of a death benefit from specific accounts (like life insurance policies, bank accounts, IRAs, etc.) to the child who received less. Alternatively, you could set up a new account solely for that child. This approach allows your will to treat all children equally in its primary provisions while still providing a means to balance the scales discreetly. This way, you can avoid potential feelings of inequity among your children while still addressing past disparities in financial support.

4. Social Media Planning

Over the past decade, I have consistently captured and shared snapshots of my family's milestones and everyday joys across Facebook, Instagram, and TikTok. A key highlight has been revisiting these moments, particularly through Facebook Memories, which has significantly contributed to my ongoing engagement with these platforms. These digital memories are not mere posts; they are cherished intangible assets that unite my family, igniting both laughter and tears as we reminisce. Nonetheless, the question of what becomes of my social media accounts and the broader scope of my digital legacy—including the extensive hours spent writing books, articles, notes on Google Drive, and various projects on YouTube—after my passing remains a concern shared by many.

The lasting value of digital memories became profoundly clear to me following my interactions with two significant figures in my life, Brian Oldroyd and Kree Anderson. Brian, a cherished high school friend, stayed connected through Facebook and Instagram, our exchanges filled with shared humor and a sense of camaraderie. His passing last year from cancer made me revisit his page, where scrolling through his posts and our Instagram DMs evoked a vivid sense of his ongoing presence through his distinct humor.

Similarly, Kree Anderson, my missionary companion in Ituy among the headhunting Igorot tribes of Luzon Island, played a pivotal role in my life, to the extent that I dedicated a book to our shared experiences. The loss felt upon discovering that Kree's Facebook page had been deactivated posthumously, coupled with a phone update erasing our text history, devastating me and underscored the impermanence of digital connections.

These individuals were more than friends; they were mentors who left an indelible mark on my life. Kree embodied courage, while Brian's kindness was akin to what some might describe as Christ-like love. Recognizing the irreplaceable value of their social media accounts as estate planning attorney, I see these platforms as vital to preserving memories and maintaining connections that transcend the physical realm.

Addressing the common skepticism of "Why should I care, I'll be dead?" necessitates a reflection on the lasting impact our absence has on those we leave behind. This very question underscores the essence of my book, emphasizing the importance of mindful preparation for the inevitable. The profound sense of loss experienced with the passing of close friends, coupled with the permanent erasure of shared memories, starkly illustrates the void left in the wake of our departure.

To safeguard the accessibility of your social media accounts—and the invaluable memories they encapsulate—for your loved ones, it is imperative to act proactively. A pragmatic step involves compiling a comprehensive list of your social media usernames and passwords, and entrusting this information to your executor or a designated family member. This preemptive measure ensures the preservation of your digital legacy, offering continued comfort and a sense of connection to those who hold you dear.

The fate of your social media accounts after your passing is determined by the policies of each platform. For instance, Facebook has established specific guidelines for handling accounts posthumously.

 Facebook's Legacy Contact and Memorialization Process

Facebook allows users to designate a Legacy Contact, a digital equivalent of naming a beneficiary, to manage their account after death. Setting up a Legacy Contact involves the following steps:

1. Navigate to Facebook's Account Settings.
2. Choose 'Memorialization Settings.'
3. Select a Legacy Contact and provide the necessary permissions.

Memorialized accounts offer a way for friends and family to gather, share, and reminisce about the departed. Features of these accounts include:

- The addition of "Remembering" next to the person's name.
- Friends can share memories on the timeline, depending on privacy settings.
- The profile and shared content remain visible to the original audience.
- Memorialized accounts do not appear in public spaces like suggestions or advertisements.
- It's not possible to log into a memorialized account, and accounts without a Legacy Contact cannot be modified.

A Legacy Contact can make limited updates to the memorialized account, such as changing profile pictures and accepting friend requests. However, the core content of the account remains unchanged.

Access Without Being a Legacy Contact

If you're not a Legacy Contact but need access to a memorialized account, you must be legally recognized as the executor or administrator of the deceased's estate. This process varies by jurisdiction and may require:

1. With a Will: The named executor must obtain formal probate court approval and receive "Letters Testamentary" to act on behalf of the estate.

2. Without a Will: The probate court will appoint an administrator, typically a close relative, who must also receive court approval and "Letters of Administration" to manage the estate.

Duties of Executors and Administrators

Both executors and administrators are tasked with estate management, including securing assets, settling debts, and distributing the estate in accordance with the will or state law. They must also adhere to legal requirements and deadlines specific to their jurisdiction.

 Instagram's Approach to Accounts After a User Passes Away

Instagram's policy for handling accounts of deceased users diverges from Facebook's by not offering a legacy contact option. Instead, Instagram provides two main paths: memorialization or deletion of the account.

Memorialization of Accounts:

Memorialized accounts on Instagram are designed to serve as a tribute to the deceased, allowing their digital legacy to remain accessible.

- Memorialized accounts are locked and cannot be logged into.
- The word "Remembering" appears next to the person's name on their profile.
- Posts shared by the deceased, including photos and videos, remain visible to the audience they were shared with.
- These accounts do not appear in public spaces like the Explore page.
- No changes can be made to the account's existing content or settings.

For memorialization requests, Instagram directs users to its Help Center for more information.

Deleting the Account:

Instagram advises downloading a copy of the account's data before deletion, as access to Instagram's Data Download tool is unavailable post-deletion. This step is critical for preserving the digital memories of the deceased.

The Potential Risks and Limitations of Social Media Account Memorialization:

1. Probate and Legacy Contact Limitations: The absence of a Legacy Contact for Facebook accounts necessitates probate proceedings to manage the deceased's digital assets, complicating the inheritance of social media accounts.

2. Restricted Access to Business Accounts: Memorialization restricts access to the deceased's business-related social media operations, potentially disrupting ongoing business activities.

3. Revenue Loss Concerns: Programs requiring active login, like the Instagram Creator Incentive Program, are inaccessible once an account is memorialized, potentially leading to financial losses.

4. Impact on Business Marketing and Operations: The inability to update or interact with a memorialized account can severely affect a business's online strategy and growth.

5. Legal and Practical Challenges: Understanding and navigating the memorialization process involves legal complexities and requires careful planning to ensure the deceased's digital legacy is appropriately managed.

Given these challenges, it is essential for individuals and businesses to proactively consider the management of their social media accounts in their estate planning, incorporating strategies such as designating a Legacy

Contact where possible and ensuring their digital assets are accounted for in their estate plans.

X (Twitter) Policy for Deceased User Accounts

X (Twitter) facilitates the deactivation of accounts belonging to deceased users, allowing authorized persons or immediate family members to request account removal. Notably, X (Twitter) simplifies this process by not mandating estate probate as a prerequisite.

To initiate a deactivation request, one must reach out to X (Twitter) with the necessary documentation. Upon submission, X (Twitter) outlines subsequent steps via email, which include providing details of the deceased, the requester's identification, and the death certificate of the deceased. This stringent process ensures the prevention of unauthorized or fraudulent requests, maintaining the confidentiality and integrity of the information provided.

It's crucial to understand that X (Twitter) does not permit account access to family members or estate administrators; access to the deceased's account requires the individual's login details. This policy underscores X (Twitter)'s commitment to privacy and security, emphasizing the importance of pre-planning digital legacies to ensure the preservation and management of digital content beyond one's lifetime.

LinkedIn's Procedure for Handling Accounts of Deceased Members

To address the passing of a LinkedIn member, LinkedIn Support requires notification with the deceased's detailed information, including the date of death and an obituary link. Closing the account necessitates legal documentation, typically Letters Testamentary, Letters of Administration, or Letters of Representation, to establish authority.

LinkedIn also provides an option to memorialize the account, transforming the profile into a lasting homage to the deceased's professional life. This allows the professional community to acknowledge and remember the deceased's contributions and achievements.

When deciding between memorialization and closure of a LinkedIn account, it's essential to consider the platform's role in representing the professional identity and legacy of the deceased. Such a decision should align with the deceased's wishes for their professional digital footprint.

Planning for digital legacy is imperative, encouraging individuals to communicate their preferences for posthumous online presence management. This ensures that one's digital legacy is treated in accordance with their wishes, reflecting the importance of thoughtful digital estate planning.

 Managing a Deceased User's Google Account

Google accounts play a central role in our digital lives, serving as the foundation for platforms like YouTube and as repositories for vast amounts of personal data. To address concerns about digital legacy, Google introduced the Inactive Account Manager feature. This allows individuals to designate a trusted contact to manage their account should it become inactive for a predefined duration, enabling proactive digital legacy planning.

If you're not designated as the Inactive Account Manager for a deceased user's Google account, Google provides a process to request access or closure of the account. This involves submitting detailed information and documentation to confirm your relationship to the deceased and justify your request, ensuring a respectful and secure handling of digital legacies.

Google's approach underscores the importance of deliberate planning for digital assets. By utilizing tools like the Inactive Account Manager, individuals can dictate the management of their digital footprints, simplifying the process for loved ones to honor their wishes posthumously.

 **Handling a TikTok Account After a User's Death**

TikTok's policy regarding deceased users' accounts differs from other social media platforms, with no formal procedures for memorialization or account deletion requests by family members. The only method to delete an account is through a direct request by the account holder or someone with login credentials.

Key points regarding TikTok's policy include:

1. Lack of Memorialization Options: TikTok does not mark accounts with a memorial status nor does it allow for account deletion by next of kin without access credentials.

2. Username Changes for Inactive Accounts: TikTok may reassign usernames of inactive accounts, altering them to a sequence of numbers after extended inactivity, though previously published content remains accessible.

For accounts associated with the TikTok Creativity Program, managing posthumous account details and revenue necessitates access to the account. Without direct access, legal consultation or exploring alternative methods may be required to manage or redirect any generated income appropriately.

Planning for Your TikTok Account:

1. Casual Users: Individuals using TikTok for personal enjoyment should consider the legacy of their digital content, as their account remains unchanged after death.

2. Business Accounts: For TikTok users operating business accounts, it's crucial to plan for account management to prevent potential risks associated with prolonged inactivity, such as identity theft or loss of business assets. In addition, loss of revenue from bonuses can occur if your

These guidelines highlight the need for thoughtful consideration and planning regarding the management of digital assets, ensuring that one's digital legacy is preserved and protected according to their wishes.

5. History of Wills

Wills have been created by humans since the inception of writing. One of the oldest known wills in existence is a fascinating artifact that transports us back to ancient Egypt, specifically to the town of Deir el-Medina, the village of the craftsmen who built the tombs in the Valley of the Kings. This document dates back to the Twentieth Dynasty, around 1150 BCE, under the reign of Pharaoh Ramesses III. The will belongs to a workman named Naunakhte, and it provides a unique glimpse into the lives, legal practices, and societal values of ancient Egyptian civilization.

The Discovery and Content of Naunakhte's Will

Naunakhte's will was discovered among the papyri in Deir el-Medina, an area renowned for its wealth of archaeological findings that shed light on the daily lives of the people who lived there. The village itself was home to

51

a literate community of artisans and workers employed in the construction and decoration of the royal tombs, which explains the presence of such a document in this location.

Naunakhte's will is notable not only for its age but also for the insight it offers into the personal and familial dynamics of the time. In her will, Naunakhte made specific bequests to her children, dividing her possessions among them. However, what makes her will extraordinary is the clear expression of her personal wishes regarding which of her children were to inherit and which were not, based on their treatment of her in her old age[5].

Naunakhte specified that those of her children who had cared for her and shown her kindness were to receive a portion of her estate, while those who had neglected her were explicitly disinherited. This decision underscores the importance of filial duty and the expectation of reciprocal care within families, a value deeply ingrained in Egyptian society.

The existence of Naunakhte's will highlights the sophistication of ancient Egyptian legal practices related to estate planning and succession. It demonstrates that women in ancient Egypt could own property and had the legal right to distribute their possessions as they saw fit upon their death. The will was executed with the presence of witnesses, indicating a formal legal process that ensured the deceased's wishes were respected and carried out.

Moreover, the document reflects the societal norms and values of the time, particularly the emphasis on family responsibilities and the moral

---

[5] Černý, Jaroslav. "The Will of Naunakhte and the Related Documents." *Journal of Egyptian Archaeology* 31 (1945): 29-53.

judgments that could affect one's inheritance. It provides a rare and personal look into how justice, familial duty, and personal relationships intertwined in the legal and social fabric of ancient Egyptian life.

Wills Are Not Universal Allowed

Throughout history, the concept of wills and the freedom to distribute one's property after death has not been a universal right. Various cultures and legal systems have imposed restrictions on this practice, reflecting differing views on property, family obligations, and societal harmony. This section explores the historical contexts in which some nations did not allow individuals to create wills, highlighting the diverse approaches to succession and inheritance.

In some societies, the concept of collective ownership, particularly among indigenous peoples and communal societies, minimized the individual's role in distributing property upon death. These cultures often emphasized the collective welfare and continuity of the group over individual property rights. For instance, among many Native American tribes, the idea of personal property was fluid, and belongings were considered to belong to the community as a whole. In such contexts, the European concept of a will, designed to distribute individual assets, was largely irrelevant and unrecognized.

Feudal systems in medieval Europe and clan-based societies in places like Scotland and Japan had their own rules governing the succession of titles, lands, and duties, which often left little room for personal testamentary freedom. In feudal Europe, the lord of the manor had significant control over land tenure, and inheritance was typically governed by primogeniture (the right of the eldest son to inherit) or other forms of customary law rather than individual wills. Similarly, in clan-based societies, the leadership and land were passed down according to clan rules, focusing on preserving the power and continuity of the clan rather than individual preference.

In absolute monarchies, where the sovereign's word was law, the distribution of property could be tightly controlled by the monarchy or the state, leaving little room for personal testamentary dispositions. For example, in Tsarist Russia before the reforms of Peter the Great, the will of the monarch could significantly influence the distribution of lands and titles, overshadowing individual wishes.

Religious laws have also played a role in restricting the practice of will-making. In some Islamic societies, for example, the Islamic law of inheritance (Sharia) specifies fixed shares for heirs, leaving a limited portion of one's estate (up to one-third) that can be disposed of by will. This system aims to ensure a fair and equitable distribution among family members according to religious principles, thus limiting the individual's ability to freely distribute their entire estate through a will.

In the 20th century, socialist and communist regimes often imposed strict controls over property rights, negating the need or legality of personal wills for the distribution of property. In these systems, the state controlled most or all property, and the concept of private inheritance was either severely restricted or abolished altogether. The ideological underpinning was that wealth and resources should be distributed according to the needs of the community or state rather than individual desires.

The restrictions on will-making in various societies throughout history reflect a complex interplay of cultural, legal, religious, and ideological factors. These systems prioritized collective interests, familial continuity, religious mandates, or state control over individual testamentary freedom. Understanding these diverse perspectives enriches our appreciation of the varied approaches to succession and inheritance across cultures and eras, highlighting the intricate balance between individual rights and societal values.

Roman Contributions, Medieval Period and Common Law Tradition

Roman law introduced several key concepts in the realm of wills, including the notions of testamentary capacity, the role of witnesses, and the executor—a person designated to carry out the wishes of the deceased. These innovations laid the foundation for modern wills, emphasizing the importance of clear intentions and legal procedures in succession planning.

The fall of the Roman Empire led to a period where the Church assumed greater control over the legal aspects of daily life, including succession. During the medieval period, wills were often executed in ecclesiastical courts, and bequests to the Church were encouraged, reflecting the intertwined nature of spiritual welfare and earthly possessions. This era underscored the role of wills in societal and religious contexts, highlighting the evolving interplay between personal desires and communal norms.

The development of common law in England marked a significant shift in the history of wills. The Statute of Wills in 1540 was a landmark moment, granting individuals greater freedom in directing the distribution of their estates, independent of feudal obligations or royal interests. This legal evolution mirrored broader societal changes, including the rise of individual rights and the gradual secularization of succession laws.

Conclusion: The Enduring Significance of Wills

The history of wills reflects the complexities of human societies, their laws, and their values. From ancient codifications to modern statutes, wills have served as a vital mechanism for expressing personal autonomy, safeguarding family interests, and transmitting cultural and material legacies across generations. As we continue to navigate the challenges of the 21st century, the evolution of wills remains a testament to the enduring human desire to shape our posthumous legacy, ensuring that our values, wishes, and assets are passed down in accordance with our deepest convictions.

6: Will Formalities

In estate planning, there are three primary types of wills: the **formal will**, the **holographic will**[6], and the **nuncupative will**[7]. In Texas, only formal and holographic wills are recognized. A formal will is a written document witnessed by others, but it does not require notarization. A holographic will, on the other hand, is entirely written in the testator's own handwriting and does not need witnesses.

---

[6] Texas Estate Code 251.052 allows an exception to the formality of the subscribing witnesses to a will if "a will [is] written wholly in the testator's handwriting."

[7] An oral **will** (or **nuncupative will**) is a **will** that has been delivered orally (that is, in speech) to witnesses, as opposed to the usual form of wills, which is written and according to a proper format.

In my practice, issues related to the proper execution of wills occasionally arise. There are three main concerns to consider when selecting witnesses for a will:

(1) the role of the witnesses during the signing,

(2) the required number of witnesses, and

(3) the criteria for a credible witness.

Witnesses are tasked with observing the signing and assessing whether the testator appears mentally capable of making a will. Since witnesses are typically not medical professionals, their role is to observe and apply their best judgment. Most states require two witnesses, although a few may require three. It's advisable to check the specific requirements of your state.

Determining who qualifies as a credible witness is more nuanced. In Texas, a "credible witness" is equivalent to a "competent witness." Legally, this means someone who does not stand to gain financially from the will's provisions. Therefore, it's important not to use family members as witnesses if they are beneficiaries of the will, as this could compromise the will's validity and potentially lead to legal challenges.

Wills Must Go Through Probate

Many clients believe that creating a will exempts their estate from undergoing probate. However, this is a misconception. In reality, for a will to be deemed valid, it must pass through the probate process. It may seem counterintuitive, but a will only gains legal validity once a judge has formally admitted it to probate, a step that occurs posthumously. This underscores the importance of understanding that the existence of a will does not bypass the probate process; rather, it is an integral part of validating and executing the decedent's wishes.

Holographic Will Saved The Day

"Did your husband make a will?"

"No, we just never got around to it," Mary confessed regretfully. Her husband, to whom she had been married for 25 years, had recently passed away after a prolonged 15-year struggle with chronic illness. Mary was the sole breadwinner, but in Texas, being a community property state, her husband retained a 50% interest in their home. This property was Mary's primary asset.

"Without a will from your husband, and given he had children from a previous relationship, his half of the property would typically pass to his children," I explained. Mary, having done her research, was aware of this but had hoped for a different outcome.

Curiously, I noticed Mary was holding a substantial file. "What's in there?" I inquired. Inside, I found several pages of her late husband's handwritten notes. Among them might be the very thing we needed—a holographic will. I carefully examined a note that read, "When I'm dead, I give everything to my wife…" The presence of his signature, Jason Bradley, at the bottom sparked hope.

Navigating through some legal complexities, we were able to submit Jason Bradley's handwritten document as his valid last will and testament. This crucial piece of evidence effectively bequeathed the entire property to Mary, providing her with the freedom to continue living there or to sell it as she saw fit.

Why is it Important to Understand?

In order to create a will, a person must have:
- legal capacity,[8]
- testamentary capacity,[9]
- testamentary intent, and[10]
- compliance with state formalities.

Contested wills often revolve around two primary issues: doubts about the testator's testamentary capacity and non-compliance with state formalities for will creation.

Wilma had been a longtime client of mine. Each year, she would visit my office to revise her will, habitually noting her desired changes directly on the document itself. I consistently warned her that writing on the will could inadvertently invalidate it, but she struggled to remember this advice. Although Wilma's mental acuity had declined, she still possessed the testamentary capacity needed to make a will. In each of our meetings, she understood that she was amending her will, grasped its implications, and could identify her children. However, her capability waned noticeably during our final meeting.

---

[8] A person's authority under law to engage in a particular task, like creating a will.
[9] Testamentary capacity is the legal term used to describe a person's legal and mental ability to make or alter a valid will.
[10] Testamentary intent is the testator's intention to create a will.

During this last visit, Wilma was accompanied by her son, Chris, who appeared disheveled and spoke on her behalf throughout the appointment. Concerned, I requested a private conversation with Wilma to ascertain her genuine intentions. Once alone with her, it became clear that she was no longer the astute woman I had known in her early 90s. Without Chris's presence, she seemed disoriented and confused, lacking the necessary testamentary capacity to revise her will. Ethically and legally, I couldn't proceed with any changes.

Years later, after Wilma's passing, an attorney representing her other children contacted me. It emerged that following our last meeting, Chris had taken his mother to a different attorney, where she signed a new will and a deed, leaving everything to Chris. This new will became the subject of protracted legal battles, which, to my knowledge, are still unresolved. This case serves as a poignant reminder of the complexities and potential issues surrounding will creation, especially in the presence of declining mental capacity.

Tips and Tricks - Adopted Children

In Texas and several other states, an adopted child retains the right to inherit from their biological parents. Recently, a man visited my office, believing he was the sole beneficiary of his father's estate. Upon inquiring if his father had other children, he mentioned a sister who was adopted away at birth. I advised him to locate and present her adoption papers to the court, to demonstrate that her inheritance rights were legally terminated.

This situation frequently arises in the context of clearing the title to a property. It's imperative to inform your estate planning attorney about all biological and adopted children to ensure accurate and comprehensive estate planning. This information is crucial in determining the rightful heirs and in avoiding potential disputes or legal complications in the future.

7. History of Trusts

A trust is a fiduciary arrangement where a "trustor" or "settlor" entrusts another party, called the "trustee," with the responsibility to manage assets or property for the benefit of a third party, termed the "beneficiary." Tracing the origins of this concept deep into history is challenging, but evidence suggests that the practice of separating equitable interest from legal interest has long been used to ensure proper management and preservation of property and power. This separation is fundamental to the trust structure, allowing for efficient and responsible administration of assets across generations or according to specific conditions set by the trustor. However, this legal concept took shape over thousands of years.

Oldest Known Precursor to Trust Law

The Gortyn Code of Crete, dating back to 480 BC, is one of the earliest known separations of beneficial and legal interest in property. This ancient legal code provides fascinating insights into the early concepts of property rights and management that bear a resemblance to modern trust principles.

In the Gortyn Code, specific regulations were laid out regarding the management of property after the death of a wife. According to these laws, a husband was obligated to manage his deceased wife's assets, but he had to do so for the benefit of their offspring. This stipulation created a division of rights and responsibilities concerning the property—a bifurcation that is fundamentally similar to the structure of a trust in contemporary law.

In the context of modern trusts, there is typically a separation between the legal title (ownership) of an asset and its beneficial use. The trustee holds the legal title to the property, but they must manage and use it for the benefit of the beneficiaries, not for their own personal gain. Similarly, in the Gortyn Code, the husband, upon his wife's death, assumed a role akin to that of a trustee. He held legal control over the property but was required to manage it in a way that respected the rights and interests of their children, the beneficiaries in this context.

Thus, the Gortyn Code of Crete stands as a significant historical precursor to modern trust law, reflecting an early comprehension of concepts like fiduciary responsibility, the separation of legal control and beneficial interest, and the protection of beneficiaries' rights—all of which are integral to the trust structures we use today.

Although the Gortyn Code appears to mark the genesis of trusts, its concept did not proliferate globally. Instead, the legal and equitable interests in property were predominantly retained by the beneficiary. This arrangement aligns more closely with the functions of a power of attorney or a financial guardianship rather than those of a trustee. To understand this better, let's examine some examples.

Advisors: Distinct from Trustees

In the final years of Emperor Gaozu's reign over the Han dynasty, a dramatic scene of political intrigue unfolded within the palace walls. The emperor's favor shifted from Empress Lü Zhi to his concubine, Qi, igniting a crisis over the imperial succession. His son with Lü Zhi, Liu Ying, the rightful heir, was deemed too feeble to rule. Gaozu contemplated replacing him with his son from Concubine Qi, Liu Ruyi. Sensing her son's perilous position, Empress Lü Zhi consulted Zhang Liang, a trusted advisor, who suggested seeking wisdom from the Four Whiteheads of Mount Shang, respected figures of moral authority.

In 195 BC, as Gaozu's health waned and his resolve to replace Liu Ying strengthened, influential voices like Shusun Tong and Zhou Chang protested, but to no avail. Then, the Four Whiteheads arrived, pledging to guide Liu Ying if he remained the heir. Their support swayed the emperor, who eventually upheld Liu Ying's position, thereby preserving the dynasty's stability.

Indeed, the story of the Four Whiteheads in the context of the Han dynasty does highlight an early form of advisory role that, while not a trust in the legal sense, shares some conceptual similarities with the foundational ideas of trusts. The Four Whiteheads, acting as advisors, had no legal claim or interest in the right to rule the kingdom, which is a key distinction from a trust where legal title to property or assets is held by one party for the benefit of another.

In the case of the Four Whiteheads, their role was more about providing counsel and guidance to ensure the welfare and stability of the kingdom, which is akin to the advisory role a trustee might play. While not a trust in the technical sense, this historical example shows how ancient societies recognized and valued the importance of separating personal interests from advisory or stewardship roles, a principle that is a precursor to the more structured legal concept of trusts that developed later.

Many clients believe that simply appointing someone "in charge" effectively establishes a trust. However, this action may result in something resembling a trust or perhaps something akin to the advisory structure seen in the Han Dynasty. Crucial to the formation of a legitimate trust is the development and understanding of the legal interest vested in the advisor or trustee.

Hope Alone Does Not Establish a Trust

In the year 195 BC—the very same year that saw Gaozu wrestling with his paternal quandary—a seminal figure was born as a slave to Terentius Lucanus. Publius Terentius Afer, commonly known in the English tongue as Terence, an African Roman playwright, with such profound talent Lucanus freed him at a young age. Within the folds of his dramatic work lay one of antiquity's earliest expositions on the concept of Fideicommissa:

"Oh Mysis, Mysis, indelibly etched upon my soul is the dying wish of Chrysis concerning Glycerium," so wrote Terence, a former African slave, in a work that transcends time as an immortal piece of dramatic literature. On her deathbed, Chrysis beseeches Pamphilus, saying, "Behold the frailty of beauty and youth, fragile shields against impropriety and loss. In the

name of your solemn pledges, your innermost integrity, and your honor—
I bequeath to you the role of husband, friend, guardian, and father. All our earthly possessions I consign to your stewardship, confiding in your honorable nature."

Terence's "Andria," adapted in 166 BC from two earlier plays by Menander—Samia and Perinthia—was his first public performance. It later garnered the distinction of being the earliest of Terence's plays to be staged in the Renaissance, in Florence in 1476. This reinforces the maxim that trust serves as the bedrock of all relationships[11].

In delving into the ancient roots of "The Woman from Andros," one uncovers a truth that transcends time: the art of entrusting property for the benefit of another is as old as civilization itself. Menander, the Athenian playwright, had already explored these themes a century before Terence. In the city-states of ancient Greece, this method was not merely an alternative to inheritance; it was the favored mechanism.

However, mere hope is insufficient to establish a trust. Consider the case of Tim Blair, a fictional name for storytelling purposes. He came to my office one afternoon as the designated beneficiary of his mother's bank account, which held investments totaling approximately $300,000. On her deathbed, she had expressed her wishes to him, saying, "I left it for you to do what is best for your siblings." The responsibility visibly weighed on him. He found himself in control of an amount more significant than he had ever accumulated in his life, an amount five times his annual salary, meant to be distributed among six people. He departed from my office immersed in contemplation. That was the last time I saw him.

---

[11] Broughton, Thomas Robert Shannon. *The Magistrates of the Roman Republic.* American Philological Association, 1986

Absolute Division of Interest

Sold into slavery by his brothers, Joseph rose to become the Vizier of Egypt, a position of immense power and responsibility. As Vizier, he was not just a high-ranking official but also a steward of the Pharaoh's resources and a protector of the Egyptian people. His role in managing the kingdom's granaries during a time of famine is a testament to the trust placed in him and his fulfillment of fiduciary duties. This story, transcending its religious context, laid the conceptual groundwork for the legal notion of managing assets for the benefit of others.

The role of a Vizier in ancient Egypt was multifaceted, serving as an advisor, administrator, and confidant to the Pharaoh. Their position was akin to that of a trustee, as they managed state affairs, provided guidance, and ensured the welfare of the kingdom, without having personal claims to the throne. This role highlighted the importance of impartiality, integrity, and the prioritization of others' interests — key elements of fiduciary responsibility.

However, Joseph's role was not equivalent to that of a trustee, as he lacked the authority to be considered one. His position was more akin to that of a Power of Attorney. He acted on behalf of the Pharaoh, without holding any personal interest in the property. A trustee, in contrast, is vested with actual legal rights over the trust's assets. A Power of Attorney, similar to a Vizier, is authorized to act as a representative of the principal, but does not possess the same level of legal ownership or control over assets as a trustee does.

Reviving the Trust: The Initial Steps in Creation of a Legal Process for Disputes

In Roman law, the concept of fiduciary duty evolved from the legal institution known as fideicommissum. This was a significant step in codifying the idea of entrusting property for the benefit of another. Fideicommissum allowed a testator to leave property to a beneficiary (the fiduciary), with the understanding that the beneficiary would then convey it to a third party (the final recipient), often under specified conditions. This mechanism was particularly useful in situations where direct inheritance was not possible or desirable due to legal constraints or personal preferences.

The development of fideicommissum reached a pivotal moment under the reign of Antoninus Pius, a Roman Emperor known for his legal reforms and dedication to administrative efficiency. Antoninus Pius recognized the practical and moral value of fideicommissum, leading to its formal codification in Roman law. His contributions ensured that the system was more systematically applied and legally recognized, providing a framework for future generations to manage and transfer property with a sense of moral obligation and legal responsibility.

Antoninus Pius' codification of fideicommissum marked a crucial point in the history of estate planning and property management. It established a legal precedent for the concept of trusts and laid the foundation for the evolution of modern fiduciary law. His work demonstrated an understanding of the complexities of inheritance and property rights, and his efforts to formalize fideicommissum were a testament to the enduring importance of trust and stewardship in managing assets for the benefit of others.

The Rebirth of the Trust

King Henry VIII confronted the emergence of "Uses." During the early 16th century, English common law imposed stringent regulations concerning land inheritance. Traditionally, land would exclusively transfer to the eldest son, known as the "heir-at-law," leaving little room for maneuvering. Nevertheless, individuals sought greater authority in determining the beneficiaries of their property. Their objectives encompassed providing for daughters, younger sons, and even illegitimate children, a group frequently marginalized by the prevailing common law principles.

To get around these limitations, landowners started using the concept of "uses." They would transfer the legal title of their land to a trusted individual, known as a "feoffee," who would hold the land "to the use" of someone else, often as specified in the landowner's will. This allowed landowners to effectively control who benefited from their land after their death, bypassing the rigid common law rules.

This practice had financial implications for the Crown. Under the feudal system, the Crown had certain financial rights over land when it was inherited. For example, the Crown could claim the profits from an heir's land until the heir came of age. This was a significant source of income for the Crown.

However, because "uses" allowed landowners to sidestep the traditional rules of inheritance, the Crown was losing out on these revenues. The land was not technically being "inherited" in the way that would trigger these

70

feudal payments; it was simply being managed by the feoffee for the benefit of someone else.

To protect its financial interests, the Crown took legislative action. Laws were enacted to regulate the use of "uses" and ensure that the Crown could still collect its due revenues. These interventions aimed to balance the flexibility that "uses" offered to landowners with the financial needs of the Crown, ultimately leading to the more formalized system of trusts that we have today.

Today, the trust continues to be an essential element in estate planning. The necessity of having a reliable person to carry out your wishes, and the means to empower them to do so, has developed over time. This evolution spans from the biblical figure Joseph, through the Han dynasty's succession challenges, to the dramatic works of Terence, and onto significant legal advancements in both ancient Rome and medieval England. Trust is not just about transferring property; it's about the continuity of legacies, stewardship, and the assurance that one's wishes will be honored. In contemporary society, this principle is upheld through legal frameworks that hold fiduciaries and trustees accountable, ensuring that the architecture of legacies endures beyond one's lifetime.

8: Trust Purpose

The essence of a Trust is straightforward. It is established when it proves advantageous for an individual or entity to oversee property on behalf of another. This arrangement grants the Trustee legal authority to manage the assets for the Beneficiary's advantage. The pivotal question, however, concerns the circumstances under which it becomes preferable to entrust property management to another for someone's benefit. These scenarios are explored in detail in Part 3. To illustrate this concept further, I'll share an experience of advising a client on the necessity of creating a trust for his daughter.

"Mr. Willingham, I'm a simple man. I don't want anything complicated like one of those trusts. I just want my son to take care of my daughter after I pass away. My daughter has Down's and I want to make sure that what I leave will take care of her."

I knew I had my work cut out for me. It's difficult to explain to clients that things aren't always as simple as they seem. "I understand, and I'll make this as simple as possible, but what you are explaining is a trust. Whenever you put someone in charge of another person's property, you are creating a trust."

Mr. Freddrick looked at me like I was trying to rip him off. He had dealt with an attorney in the past, and it was not a good experience. In addition, the trust his father created was so outdated that when his father passed away, it seemed to be more trouble than it was worth. I had seen his father's trust, and I knew about its weak spots.

"I know you are not a fan of your father's trust. Your father created a trust for a very different reason from why you are here today. Your father created a trust for estate tax issues. You need a trust to protect your daughter. While both are trusts, the purpose and structure are much different." I had his attention, but I still needed him to understand that no two trusts are identical.

I took a handful of pens out of the cup on my desk. "Property law can be understood as a bundle of pens. Each pen is a "right." One pen might be the right to manage property; another pen might be the right for property to benefit you. Anytime we separate the right to manage from the right to benefit, we create a trust. Your father did this in order to allow time to pursue an exclusion amount for estate tax purposes. He gave his wife the right to hold legal title but gave his children the beneficial right. What you want isn't so different. You want to give your son legal right to hold property and your daughter the beneficial right. Is that correct?"

Mr. Freddrick was warming up to me but still felt like I was trying to sell him an expensive trust. "Why can't I just leave my property to my son, and he'll just take care of it for Anna?" This is a great question. In his mind, this would avoid the need, the cost, and the effort of a trust.

"My clients ask this question all the time. There are a few things that can go wrong. First, your son could die before your daughter, and all that money would pass according to his estate planning documents. Second, if your son ended up in a nursing home, Medicaid would penalize him for a fraudulent transfer. Third, if your son were sued, his creditors or the IRS could take all the money. Fourth, your son might not be able to handle the pressure of doing the right thing and might keep the money for himself. At least in a trust, we can enforce fiduciary duties upon your son. Besides, he would have to create a trust anyway, so it's better to handle it now."

Mr. Freddrick was coming around to the idea that a trust could be useful in his situation. "One other benefit that a trust could provide is to help shelter your daughter's inheritance from a Medicaid lien. We could create a supplemental needs trust for your daughter so that she can qualify for government benefits."

Mr. Freddrick liked all the extra benefits of the trust, but he did not want to spend any more money than he had planned before coming to my office. I told him he could always come back and do it later. We left with him telling me that he would come back and get a trust later; I have not seen him. Hopefully, he gets back in before it is too late.

Settlors, Trustees, and Beneficiaries

Clients often find the terminology surrounding trusts perplexing, especially when it comes to the roles of various individuals involved. A trust typically involves three key players: the Settlor, the Trustee, and the Beneficiary. Additional roles, like a Trust Protector or an Appointer, might also be part of the trust structure. Each of these roles is vital for the trust's effective operation.

The Settlor

Clients sometimes wonder about the terms used in trusts. For example, the term "settlor" might seem unfamiliar. A settlor is the person who establishes the trust, dividing legal and equitable title to property and imposing fiduciary duties. This role is often fulfilled by more than one person, such as a married couple. The term "trustor" is an older term for settlor, and when a settlor splits property for tax purposes, they are typically referred to as the "grantor."

The Trustee

A common adage in estate planning is, "Being an executor or trustee is a significant responsibility." The trustee holds legal title to the trust property but does not benefit from it unless the trust stipulates a fee. Despite the absence of direct benefits, the trustee bears all the responsibilities, duties, and liabilities associated with property ownership. Accepting the role of a trustee is a serious commitment, often perceived as an honor, but it also entails substantial responsibility that can become burdensome over time.

As a trustee, you enter into a fiduciary relationship with the trust's beneficiary. This role imposes several duties, including acting in good faith, adhering to the authority granted by the trust, remaining loyal to the beneficiary, avoiding conflicts of interest, and disclosing your identity as the trustee. Trustees wield significant power, and with that power comes substantial responsibility. Any violation of trust terms or overstepping of authority can lead to legal consequences, including liability for damages or, in severe cases, criminal charges under the Texas Penal Code.

The Beneficiary

The beneficiary of a trust receives the equitable title to the property held in the trust. Sometimes referred to as the donee or grantee, the beneficiary enjoys the benefits of the trust. However, this enjoyment is subject to the conditions set by the settlor. These conditions can vary widely in their extent and duration and can even result in the forfeiture of benefits if the beneficiary violates the trust's terms. Thus, the role of a beneficiary, while beneficial, comes with its own set of limitations and obligations.

In essence, a trust empowers the settlor to impose restrictions on property for the benefit of the beneficiary, who, in accepting these benefits, agrees to abide by the terms of the trust.

Types of Trusts

Clients frequently ask about creating a trust, but the critical question for an attorney is determining the appropriate type of trust to establish. There are numerous trust varieties, each designed for specific purposes and situations. Here is a compilation of the commonly used trusts:

1. **Revocable Living Trust** - Can be altered or revoked during the grantor's lifetime.

2. **Irrevocable Trust** - Cannot be modified or revoked after a certain event.

3. **Testamentary Trust** - Established through a will and becomes effective upon death.

4. **Charitable Trust** - Established to benefit a charitable organization or cause.

5. **Charitable Remainder Trust** - Provides income to the grantor, with the remainder going to charity.

6. **Charitable Lead Trust** - A charity receives income first, with the remainder going to beneficiaries.

7. **Special Needs Trust** - Designed to benefit individuals with disabilities without disqualifying them from government assistance.

8. **Spendthrift Trust** - Protects a beneficiary's inheritance from creditors.

9. **Totten Trust** - A payable-on-death bank account acting as a trust.

10. **Bypass Trust** - Minimizes estate taxes for married couples.

11. **QTIP Trust** (Qualified Terminable Interest Property Trust) - Provides income to a surviving spouse, with the principal going to other beneficiaries after the spouse's death.

12. **Credit Shelter Trust** - Similar to a bypass trust, it shelters assets from estate tax.

13. **Grantor Retained Annuity Trust (GRAT)** - The grantor receives a fixed annuity, and beneficiaries receive the remaining assets.

14. **Grantor Retained Unitrust (GRUT)** - The grantor receives a variable annuity.

15. **Life Insurance Trust** - Holds a life insurance policy, removing it from the grantor's estate.

16. **Dynasty Trust** - Designed to last across multiple generations.

17. **Blind Trust** - The beneficiaries are unaware of the trust's assets, often used in situations to avoid conflicts of interest.

18. **Constructive Trust** - Imposed by a court to address matters of fairness or justice.

19. **Crummey Trust** - Allows for annual gifts to beneficiaries without gift tax implications.

20. **Educational Trust** - Designated for educational purposes.

21. **Family Trust** - Established to benefit family members.

22. **Generation-Skipping Trust** - Skips a generation to reduce estate taxes.

23. **Incentive Trust** - Distributes assets based on meeting certain criteria.

24. **Intentionally Defective Grantor Trust (IDGT)** - Irrevocable trust with income tax implications for the grantor.

25. **Marital Trust** - Benefits the surviving spouse.

26. **Medicaid Trust** - Helps qualify for Medicaid while preserving assets.

27. **Pet Trust** - Provides for the care of one or more pets after the owner's death.

28. **Qualified Personal Residence Trust** (QPRT) - Removes a personal residence from the estate.

29. **Rabbi Trust** - A non-qualified, deferred compensation trust for employees.

30. **Resulting Trust** - Implied by law to carry out the grantor's intent.

31. **Snowball Trust** - A Trust that purchase a life insurance policy that pays the next generation.

32. **Irrevocable Life Insurance Trust** (ILIT) - Owns life insurance policies on the grantor's life.

33. **Silent Trust** - Beneficiaries are not informed about the trust for a period.

34. **Spendthrift Provision Trust** - Protects the trust's assets from the beneficiary's creditors.

35. **Sprinkle Trust** - Trustee has discretion in how to distribute assets among beneficiaries.

36. **Standby Trust** - Activated under certain conditions, such as disability.

37. **Supplemental Needs Trust** - Similar to a special needs trust, for additional care.

38. **Tax By-Pass Trust** - Helps minimize estate taxes.

39. **Term Trust** - Lasts for a specific period.

40. **Unitrust** - Pays a fixed percentage of the trust's assets.

41. **Voting Trust** - Created to control the voting shares of a corporation.

42. **Asset Protection Trust** - Shields assets from creditors.

43. **Land Trust** - Holds real estate to conceal the owner's identity.

44. **Offshore Trust** - Established in a foreign jurisdiction for tax benefits and privacy.

45. **Pooled Income Trust** - Managed by a nonprofit for multiple beneficiaries.

46. **Purpose Trust** - Created for a specific purpose rather than to benefit individuals.

47. **Real Estate Investment Trust** (REIT) - Invests in real estate and distributes income to investors.

48. **Retirement Trust** - Manages retirement assets.

49. **Spendthrift Trust** - Protects a beneficiary's assets from creditors and their own imprudence.

50. **Qualified Income Trust** QIT- Also known as a Miller Trust, reduces income to qualify for Medicaid.

51. **Life Stage Trust** - A Trust which adapts to the development of a beneficiary.

9: Avoid Probate Without a Trust

Probate is derived from the Latin verb *probatum,* [12] "having been proven." When there is a will, probate is the judicial process to prove its validity as the testator's [13] true last will and testament. If there is no will, probate determines the heirs of an estate based on a state's intestacy laws. Below is a chart showing some of the steps taken during an uncontested probate.

In the quaint town of Flower Mound, Texas there lived an elderly gentleman named Walter Jennings. Walter, known for his wise investments

---

[12] Collins Dictionary of the English Language

[13] A testator is a creator of a will.

and considerable estate. However, upon his passing, he left behind a tangled web of assets, a will, and a family unsure of the steps ahead. The probate process began when Walter's eldest daughter, Emily, discovered his will in a well-worn leather briefcase. The will named Emily as the executor, entrusting her with the responsibility of managing the estate through probate.

Despite her grief and the recent demands of arranging her father's funeral, Emily enlisted my services to manage the legal intricacies of her father Walter's estate. Recognizing the urgency and importance of the matter, she arranged to meet with me, aware that her remaining days off were limited before she would need to use her paid time off.

Following our consultation, I promptly prepared and submitted an Application for Probate of Will and for Issuance of Letters Testamentary to the county probate court in McKinney, Texas. This key document is essential for starting the probate process, as it asks the court to validate Walter's will and approve the execution of his estate according to his final instructions.

Subsequently, I dispatched notifications to all beneficiaries, informing them about the commencement of the probate of Walter's will. This step, however, raised a significant issue for Emily, as her brother had been disinherited in the will. I advised Emily of the strong possibility that her brother might legally contest the will.

As anticipated, an attorney, Greg Hall, representing Emily's brother contacted me before the scheduled court hearing. The ensuing months were marked by legal contention. Ultimately, Emily, weary from the prolonged dispute and wishing to avoid further conflict, consented to a settlement of $300,000 to resolve her brother's challenge. This decision, she felt, was contrary to her father's intentions but necessary to bring peace and closure.

The probate court hearing proceeded as planned. At the hearing, a witness who was present during the signing of Walter's will provided testimony confirming its legitimacy. Consequently, the court officially recognized Emily as the executor of the estate, entrusting her with the authority to manage and distribute her father's assets as per the will's directives.

Emily meticulously inventoried Walter's estate, encompassing his real estate, stock portfolio, and personal items. She engaged professional appraisers to accurately value these assets, crucial for determining estate tax obligations. However, following our submission of the inventory, I was contacted by Greg Hall, representing Emily's brother, alleging deception in our valuation of the estate. This accusation led to eight months of additional legal costs. Despite my assurance of a favorable outcome in court, Emily, seeking tranquility over prolonged conflict, chose to settle once more.

With the estate properly appraised and her brother's second claim settled, Emily addressed Walter's remaining debts and taxes, utilizing the estate's resources. This step was essential in the probate process.

Then, Emily proceeded with the asset distribution to the beneficiaries according to Walter's directives. Her other siblings expressed dissatisfaction with the process's duration and unjustly accused her of misappropriation, although they stopped short of legal action. Emily diligently transferred property titles, allocated personal belongings, and ensured fair distribution to each beneficiary.

After distributing all assets, Emily submitted a final account to the probate court, documenting every action taken. The court's review and approval of this account marked the official closure of the estate.

Emily's diligent application of legal procedures led to the successful closure of Walter Jennings' estate. Regrettably, the administration of Walter Jennings' estate through probate could have been circumvented with proper estate planning, even without establishing a trust. This outcome highlights the importance of seeking professional advice in advance of one's passing.

History of Probate

The history of probate, the legal process of administering a deceased person's estate, is as ancient as the concept of personal property and land ownership. Disputes and claims over possessions following a person's death have always been a catalyst for familial discord.

One of the earliest documented instances of a probate-like process is found in the Bible, in Numbers 27:1-11. This passage describes the case of Zelophehad's daughters, who claimed their father's property upon his death, as he had no sons. Moses, acting as a judge, granted them the right to inherit, setting a precedent for inheritance rights in the absence of male heirs.

The ancient Greeks, recognizing the importance of estate distribution, allowed for the creation of wills. However, they were also aware of the potential for fraud. To mitigate this, unsealed wills were presented publicly and scrutinized for authenticity. This practice highlighted the importance of transparency and accountability in estate matters.

The Romans further developed the concept of wills and probate. They implemented various systems to manage and authenticate wills, laying foundational principles for modern probate processes. Their approach emphasized the legal and orderly transfer of property, shaping the future of estate administration.

In England, the evolution of probate saw a significant transition. Initially, the Church exerted considerable control over the distribution of personal property, while secular courts managed real estate. This dual system reflected the Church's influence on daily life and legal matters during medieval times.

As legal systems evolved, the administration of estates became more complex. The English model, influenced by common law, gradually shaped contemporary probate practices. This system balanced the need to respect the wishes of the deceased with the necessity of legal oversight to prevent fraud and ensure fair distribution.

Today, probate courts, entirely secular and government-run, still retain many features derived from historical practices. They serve as guardians of legal propriety in estate distribution, ensuring that a deceased person's assets are distributed according to their wishes, or in their absence, according to law. This evolution reflects society's ongoing effort to balance individual rights with communal responsibility in the sensitive area of inheritance.

Beneficiary Designations: A Simple Tool for Estate Planning

In estate planning, my primary aim is to keep the process as straightforward as possible. Many clients express a desire to create a trust to bypass probate, but often, simpler alternatives can be more appropriate. A key option in this regard is the use of beneficiary designations. This is particularly relevant for assets like bank accounts (both checking and savings), retirement accounts, annuities, and life insurance policies.

Understanding the nature of beneficiary designations is crucial. They represent a contractual agreement with the financial institution, dictating the transfer of the account or policy proceeds upon your passing. A common oversight in this process is not naming a contingent beneficiary, who would inherit only if the primary beneficiary is unable to do so. It's also important to dispel a prevalent misconception: a will does not override a beneficiary designation. Since the designated assets bypass the estate, they are not influenced by the terms of your will.

The efficiency of beneficiary designations is notable. On average, it takes about 20 days for a beneficiary to access funds from a designated bank account. In contrast, in the absence of such a designation, an heir may wait up to three months to access a bank account. Additionally, banks do not impose fees for transferring assets to a named beneficiary. This is in stark contrast to the expenses associated with proving a will or determining heirship, which can amount to thousands of dollars.

In summary, while trusts are a valuable tool in estate planning, beneficiary designations offer a simpler, cost-effective method to ensure the smooth transfer of certain assets, underscoring their importance in a well-rounded estate plan.

Case Study: Complexities in Life Insurance Beneficiary Designations

I encountered a peculiar case involving a dispute over the proceeds of a life insurance policy, highlighting the nuances of beneficiary designations. The opposing counsel had filed a lawsuit in federal court, claiming the proceeds should have gone to the insured's mother, even though she hadn't provided her late husband's death certificate, which was a key requirement.

Case Details:

1. **The Deceased**: The policyholder was a man without a wife or children, but with a 20-year-old girlfriend, sometimes referred to as his spouse.

2. **Beneficiary Complications**: He named this girlfriend as the primary beneficiary on his life insurance policy. After his death, she initiated the claim process but passed away before she could submit his death certificate.

3. **My Client's Role**: My client, the contingent beneficiary, was next in line according to the policy.

The policy stated:

> "**Order of Payment on the Insured's Death**. When the Insured dies, We will make payment in equal shares to the primary Beneficiaries living when payment is made. If the last primary dies, We will make payment in equal shares to the contingent Beneficiaries living when payment is made…"

The policy explicitly stated that payment would be made to living primary beneficiaries at the time of distribution. If no primary beneficiary was alive, the contingent beneficiaries would receive the proceeds. In this case, since the primary beneficiary passed away before completing the claim process, she was not "living when payment was made," thereby activating my client's claim as the contingent beneficiary.

This scenario underscores that life insurance policies are governed by their terms, not by state or federal law, wills, trusts, or any other documents. They represent a contractual agreement between the insurance company and the policyholder. Therefore, the insurer is obligated to follow the policy terms.

I've had clients who preferred not to list all their children as beneficiaries, instead leaving everything to one child with verbal instructions to distribute the assets equally among siblings. This approach can create legal complications. While a trust for real property must be in writing to be valid, a trust for personal property can be established orally. An oral agreement to distribute a bank account among children can inadvertently create a trust, leading to a challenging legal situation that could require litigation to resolve.

To avoid such complications, it's advisable to directly list all intended beneficiaries in the policy or account. This ensures clarity and adherence to your wishes without the need for additional legal interpretation or intervention.

Kim and Ron's Story: The Importance of Beneficiary Designations

Kim and Ron, in their 50s, embraced a life of adventure, selling their home, cars, and most personal belongings to travel America in an RV. However, their dream was tragically cut short when Ron suffered a massive heart attack in Melissa, Texas, leading to an eight-month battle for his life across various medical facilities. After Ron's passing, Kim faced a financial nightmare: overwhelming medical bills totaling over $900,000, much of which was not covered by Ron's insurance.

Kim, in seeking access to Ron's finances, learned from his financial advisor that she needed legal authorization. Their most significant asset was Ron's $600,000 retirement account. As I reviewed her case, it became evident that Kim wasn't the named beneficiary on Ron's account. "How long have you known your financial advisor?" I inquired, realizing the gravity of the situation. "He was Ron's best friend from college," she replied, unaware of the impending financial implications.

I explained to Kim the critical difference between accounts with and without beneficiary designations. Accounts with a beneficiary designation bypass probate and directly transfer to the named individual, avoiding creditors. However, in Ron's case, the lack of a beneficiary meant his retirement account would go through probate and be vulnerable to his medical debts. "Because there's no beneficiary listed, his retirement savings could be used to cover the $900,000 in medical bills. You might receive nothing," I told her.

During our extensive conversation, we explored various strategies to protect as much of the estate as possible through the probate process. It was a stark reminder that something as simple as a beneficiary designation form could have saved hundreds of thousands of dollars.

Financial institutions use different terms for beneficiary designations, including transfer on death (TOD), pay on death (POD), accounts with rights of survivorship, or simply beneficiary designation. Regardless of the terminology, they serve the same purpose: ensuring assets are transferred upon death contractually, outside of a will, safeguarding them from being subject to estate debts or the probate process.

Passing Real Estate Outside of Probate Without A Trust

Certain types of deeds can be used to avoid probate by making an *inter vivos* transfer of real property. The two main ways to do that in Texas are the Enhanced Life Estate Deed and the Transfer on Death Deed. Another slightly less common way is a Survivorship Deed.

Enhanced Life Estate Deed

An Enhanced Life Estate Deed or a "Lady Bird Deed" is a deed which can: (1) avoid probate by passing property to a beneficiary upon the death of the grantor, and (2) avoid the Medicaid Estate Recovery Program of Texas. The "Lady Bird Deed" received its name from Jerome Ira Solkoff. In his example, he used United States President Lyndon Johnson's wife, Claudia Alta "Lady Bird" Johnson to show how an Enhanced Life Estate Deed would work for avoiding a Medicaid Lien in Florida. The term "Lady Bird Deed," of course, was much easier to remember than Enhanced Life Estate Deed, so it stuck. Interestingly enough, Claudia Alta Johnson never did use a "Lady Bird Deed."

This particular deed allows you to transfer the ownership of your home while you retain the right to sell the property, keep the proceeds, and live in the property. Under the law, this is not considered a transfer for Medicaid or Federal Tax purposes. Therefore, you can use this deed without creating a fraudulent transfer.

Transfer on Death Deed

Effective as of September 1, 2015, Texas allows property to be transferred upon one's death through a deed known as the Transfer on Death Deed (TODD.)[14] The code specifically states that it was not intended to affect other ways of transferring property, such as the Enhanced Life Estate Deed. The following are relevant provisions of a TODD:

1. It is revocable by the grantor as long as the grantor has sufficient mental capacity;
2. It cannot be created through the use of a power of attorney;
3. It must be recorded in the county where the real property is located;
4. It does not require consideration to be effective;
5. A will does not revoke a TODD;
6. A final judgement of a court dissolving a marriage revokes a previously created TODD;
7. It does not affect ad valorem tax exemptions, including exemptions for residence homestead, persons 65 years of age or older, persons with disabilities, or veterans;
8. It does not affect an interest or right of a secured or unsecured creditor;
9. It does not affect your mother's eligibility for any public assistance;

---

[14] This law is codified under Chapter 114 of the Texas Estate Code.

10. It does not trigger the "due on sale" clause or similar clauses in a mortgage;
11. It does not invoke a statutory real estate notice or disclosure requirements;
12. It does not create a legal or equitable interest in favor of the designated beneficiary; and
13. It does not to claims or creditors of the beneficiaries.

Commonly, I get asked the question, "Should I do a TODD or an Enhanced Life Estate Deed?" As you can see above, the TODD has numerous codified benefits. As a general rule, it makes sense to use a TODD unless (1) you're going to have to sign a TODD through a power of attorney, or (2) you anticipate that you may need to revoke the TODD after a grantor has become incapacitated. All in all, the numerous codified benefits of a TODD seem to outweigh the benefits of the Enhanced Life Estate Deed.

Transfer on Death Car Title (Beneficiary Designation for a Motor Vehicle)

On September 1, 2015, The Texas State Legislature passed a law allowing for the transfer on death designation of a motor vehicle through Texas Form VTR-121 Beneficiary Designation for a Motor Vehicle.[15] As this law was passed at the same time as the Transfer on Death Deed, many individuals tend to search for this document under the name Transfer on Death Title.

---

[15] This document can be found online by going to the following link:
https://www.txdmv.gov/.../8516-vtr-121-beneficiary-designation-for-a-motor-vehicle.

A different document can be used to transfer ownership of a vehicle under rights of survivorship laws. This is Texas Form VTR-122.[16] If you have a joint owner on the vehicle, for instance a spouse, you will use this document to transfer ownership.

This new law is codified under Texas Estate Code chapter 115; below are some of the details you need to know regarding this particular law:

1. The forms are revocable;
2. A trust can be a beneficiary; (Chapter 115 uses Section 311.005 of the Government Code);
3. It is a non-probate instrument (should avoid the Medicaid Estate Recovery Program);
4. A Last Will and Testament will not revoke this beneficiary designation;
5. A beneficiary may disclaim this inheritance under chapter 240 of the Texas Property Code;
6. A spouse will have to agree to the transfer of a non-spouse;
7. A beneficiary must survive 120 hours to inherit;
8. Creditor claims still attach to property which has transferred to a beneficiary.

These two forms are simple estate planning tools that can help properly structure an estate plan.

Tips and Tricks -- Avoiding Probate

---

[16] This document can be found online by going to the following link: https://www.txdmv.gov/publications-tac/doc_download/1994-vtr-122-rights-of-survivorship-ownership-agreement-for-a-motor-vehicle.

Beneficiary designations are a valuable tool in estate planning, but they are not without limitations. A common mistake is designating a trusted family member as the beneficiary, instead of directly naming children or intended heirs. This approach is often chosen to avoid creating a trust or to prevent direct inheritance by children. The expectation is that the family member will honor the decedent's wishes and distribute the assets to the children.

However, this strategy can lead to complications. Firstly, there could be gift tax implications for the family member who receives the assets and then transfers them to the children. Secondly, and perhaps more critically, if the trusted family member passes away without properly redirecting these funds to the intended heirs, the assets will be distributed according to that person's estate plan, not the original owner's intentions. I recall a client insisting her brother would manage her estate effectively, thus negating the need for her to designate her children as beneficiaries or establish a trust. This reliance on another's estate planning, rather than taking charge of her own, posed a significant risk to her children's inheritance.

In terms of real estate, many clients worry about the complications of placing property in a trust, especially concerning refinancing. A practical solution is the use of a transfer on death deed or a similar instrument. This allows for the seamless transfer of real estate upon death. The property remains in the individual's name during their lifetime but automatically transfers to the designated beneficiary or trust upon their passing. This strategy keeps the property out of trust while the owner is alive, yet ensures it falls under the control of the trust after death, thereby streamlining the estate planning process without impeding financial flexibility during the owner's lifetime.

PART 3: REASONS TO CREATE A TRUST

10: Blended Family Nightmare

"I'm not familiar with what to do next," Cynthia sighed as we went through a probate intake. She may have spoken in broken English, but there was clearly confusion in her voice.

"That is my job. I will help you through this process," I said, smiling warmly at the young widow. Cynthia met her husband online and fell in love immediately. Richard was 62 years old with three children and a good career. Cynthia was 25 and from a small, poor village in the Philippines. The couple met, married, and had a child in a single whirlwind year. Despite his good health, Richard passed away from a heart attack. He left four children and a wife. "Let's start with this. Did your husband have a trust?"

"What is a trust?" Cynthia asked in frustration. I tried my best to converse in Tagalog, but it had been 15 years since I lived in the Philippines. Her friend had to translate.

"Did your husband have a will?"

"No."

"Unfortunately, if your husband did not have a will, almost all of his property will pass to his children. However, you do have some rights. You get a life estate in the home. You have a right to child support from his estate. You will get a ⅓ life estate in any real property that he may own." All this seemed to go over Cynthia's head.

"Will they deport me? I'm not a US citizen yet." I realized that she was not concerned about the money. She just wanted to stay in the United States.

"No. You will get to stay here." We planned out our next steps and then called it a day.

Cynthia faced continuous challenges. Upon her return a few weeks later, she discovered that his 401k policy still named his ex-wife as the beneficiary. I was compelled to explain once more that, by federal law, the 401k would be inherited by his ex-wife.

Two months later we were at the courtroom doing a prove-up hearing for a determination of heirship. In the back of the courtroom, I spotted

Richard's ex-wife. I wondered why she was at the hearing after their less-than-amicable divorce. She presented me with a will that Richard created when they were married. "I get everything. That is what the will says."

"Ma'am, a divorce terminates all of your standard inheritance rights. However, it does not terminate a will. May I have a look?" This was going to be a problem. Richard had named his ex-wife as his executor, but the divorce terminated her right to hold this position. The next in line was her father.

I took my client aside and said, "I hope we can reschedule this hearing. This might be your husband's last will, and it names his ex-wife's father as the executor of the estate. If this will is valid and there is a named executor, you will not be appointed by the court to serve as an administrator."

After an hour with the judge, he ordered another attorney in the courtroom to represent Richard's ex-wife. Over the next four months, we prepared for a contested probate. We contended that the will was in the possession of the ex-wife, so the husband would not want it probated. It was a long shot, but it was my only argument.

At the next hearing, we were able to resolve a lot of the issues except for who had the right to serve as the executor or administrator. The judge, not wanting to cause a fight, admitted the will to probate as a muniment of title[17], which allowed the trustee of the testamentary trust[18] to serve as the executor. The trustee, Richard's aunt, hired an attorney. Now there were three attorneys involved. Over the next seven months, the three of us fought for our clients. Tens of thousands of dollars were wasted on hearing after hearing, as we moved at a snail's pace.

In the end, a significant portion of the estate was consumed by attorney fees. Cynthia received very little of her husband's probatable estate, and the children's inheritance was significantly depleted. All of this would have been avoided if Richard had spent three hours of his time creating a will or a trust.

Blended Family Probate Nightmare

My office, a testament to my expertise, has witnessed numerous cases stemming from disputes in blended families. A blended family typically involves at least one spouse with a child from a previous relationship. The dynamics in such families can become complex posthumously, often due to the presence of external parties — the child from the previous relationship and their other biological parent — who may not have a vested interest in maintaining ties with the stepparent.

Intestacy laws in some states, including Texas, can complicate matters further by allocating a significant portion of a deceased spouse's estate to

---

[17] **Probate as a Muniment of Title** is a probate proceeding filed solely for the purpose of showing the heirs and to exclude opening an administration. *Munimentum* is latin, meaning written evidence of title to property. This includes deeds, wills, titles, or court judgments.

[18] Remember that a testamentary trust is a trust which is created after someone passes away through instructions in a will.

their children, rather than the surviving spouse. This legal framework can be surprising to many, so I often use diagrams to clarify these intricate legal nuances, especially for those who prefer visual aids.

Consider this scenario: If your spouse has a child with someone else, upon their death, their community property generally passes equally to their children. You, as the surviving spouse, might only receive a life estate in the real property.

Why would a law prioritize children over a spouse in property inheritance? In Texas, the intention is to protect children from previous relationships who are at risk of disinheritance once their biological parent passes away. Without a legal mandate, a surviving stepparent might favor their biological children, leaving stepchildren without an inheritance. Other states, however, adopt a different approach, presuming that a person would prefer their estate to go to their current spouse, potentially sidelining children from previous relationships.

One recurring issue I've observed is parents, particularly fathers, disinheriting their children to leave everything to a new spouse — a decision often driven by conflict avoidance rather than thoughtful planning. It's crucial to recognize that relying on a surviving spouse to include your children in their estate plan can be risky.

I recall a husband and wife who consulted me following the husband's terminal diagnosis. Despite my advice to create a trust ensuring his children's inheritance, he trusted his wife's promise to include them in her will. Tragically, within three months of his passing, she altered her will, excluding his children.

This narrative underscores the importance of proactive and deliberate estate planning in blended families. It's not only about providing for a current spouse but also about safeguarding the interests of children from previous relationships. Estate planning in such contexts should be navigated with care, foresight, and often, the guidance of a skilled attorney.

Protecting a Spouse

Most couples I speak with want to leave all their property to each other. Protecting your spouse from your greedy children is a great reason to create a trust. It's true, a will can also override state intestacy law and let you leave everything to your spouse. However, a will has to go through probate. In addition, the executor of the will has the burden to prove that it is valid.

Another issue with forgoing a trust and only creating a will is that probating a copy of a will, instead of the original document, is almost impossible in most states. The standard of proof that the testator did not destroy the original will is difficult to reach. On the other hand, most states do not require an original trust—a copy of a trust is valid unless revoked. A revocation of a trust needs to be in writing, specifically identifying the intent to revoke.

Navigating Separate Accounts in Blended Families: A Texas Perspective

In Texas, a community property state, the interplay between community property laws and inheritance can pose unique challenges in blended families. These challenges are particularly pronounced when a spouse with children from a previous marriage dies intestate (without a will). Let me illustrate this with a case I handled.

Doug, who had two daughters, Sarah and Kim, from a prior marriage, was married to Mary, his second wife, for 40 years. Upon Doug's passing without a will, Mary discovered that all of Doug's community property would go to his daughters, not to her, despite their long marriage. The couple had a joint account with rights of survivorship, totaling $350,000. In a move driven by concern, Mary transferred these funds to an account solely in her name just before Doug's death. This decision, however, led to unexpected complications.

When Sarah and Kim, represented by their attorney, demanded an accounting of Doug's estate, they discovered Mary's separate account. They argued that Doug had a community property interest in half of that account, amounting to $175,000. Mary's preemptive transfer inadvertently exposed her to a claim against these funds. Had the money remained in the joint account, Mary would have retained full rights to it upon Doug's death.

This case was a first for me, and consultations with other probate attorneys revealed it was a unique scenario. At the probate hearing, despite our argument that Mary was unaware of her survivorship rights, the judge ruled in favor of Sarah and Kim. Fortunately, we negotiated a settlement for a lower amount, but the experience underscored the complexity of separate accounts in blended families.

In summary, separate accounts in blended families can lead to significant probate challenges, especially under Texas law. It's crucial for spouses in blended families to understand the implications of how they hold and manage their assets, particularly in the context of community property and survivorship rights.

Estate Planning Strategies for Blended Families

For blended families, setting up a trust is often a critical step. The complexity of family dynamics, the potential for litigation, and the rigid nature of laws make a trust not just a recommendation, but almost a necessity. Without proper planning, the likelihood of contested probate increases, often resulting in legal expenses that erode the estate's value. Trusts can circumvent most of these conflicts, but they do require careful planning and foresight.

A common desire among couples in blended families is to leave all property to the surviving spouse. A practical strategy to balance this with the interests of children from previous relationships is through life insurance. By purchasing a life insurance policy with children named as beneficiaries, you can ensure they receive an inheritance while leaving your property, including retirement accounts and real estate, to your spouse. This approach is particularly advantageous as retirement accounts offer tax benefits for spousal transfers, and the surviving spouse often needs the family home for residence. The key is to structure the policy so that the children's inheritance is contingent on not contesting the estate, thus reducing potential conflicts.

If you are a blended family without a will, take a minute to create a holographic will[19] if you reside in a state that allows them.[20] A holographic will should be in your own handwriting. You will need to write something along the lines of, "I, [insert your name], leave all of my property to [insert the name of the person you want to leave all your property to]. In addition, I appoint, [insert name of executor] to serve as my executor independently of court oversight and without bond." After you have written this, sign it and date it. Now, call an estate planning attorney to get a proper estate plan done today.

Each of these options addresses specific needs in blended family situations, aiming to balance the rights and needs of both the surviving spouse and children from previous relationships. It's essential to tailor these strategies to your family's unique circumstances, ideally under the guidance of a skilled estate planning attorney.

---

[19] A *holographic will* is a will and testament that has been entirely handwritten and signed by the testator.

[20] The following states recognize holographic wills made within the state, though witnessing requirements vary: Alaska, Arizona, Arkansas, California, Colorado, Connecticut, Idaho, Kentucky, Louisiana, Maine, Michigan, Mississippi, Montana, Nebraska, Nevada, New Jersey, North Carolina, North Dakota, Oklahoma, Pennsylvania, South Dakota, Tennessee, Texas, Utah, Virginia, West Virginia, and Wyoming. (PLEASE CONSULT GOOGLE TO FIND THE REQUIREMENTS OF YOUR STATE).

11: Protecting Minor Children

Following the demise of his wife Pythias, Aristotle was faced with the monumental task of ensuring the future security of his minor children, Pythias the Younger and Nicomachus. In a testament to his foresight and wisdom, he meticulously crafted a will that not only protected his wealth but also laid out a detailed plan for his children's well-being. Aristotle's will explicitly stated that upon reaching marriageable age, his daughter was to wed Nicanor. Furthermore, in the event of her premature death—either before marriage or childbirth—Nicanor would inherit Aristotle's entire estate, with the liberty to manage it as he saw fit. Importantly, Nicanor was also charged with the care of both Nicomachus and Pythias the Younger, ensuring their needs were fully met in a paternal and fraternal manner.

At the time of Aristotle's death, his daughter, born to Pythias, and Nicomachus, whose mother was Herpyllis—one of Aristotle's lovers—were still minors. Aristotle, having acquired significant wealth both through inheritance and personal accumulation, appointed his nephew Nicanor not only as Pythias the Younger's future husband but also as Nicomachus's adoptive father. Nicanor's adherence to Aristotle's wishes after his passing is a testament to his loyalty. While Nicomachus's fate remains unknown, Pythias the Younger notably outlived three husbands and maintained a healthy life. Without Aristotle's proactive measures, the future of his children and his estate would have been left to chance. This highlights the timeless wisdom in appointing guardians for minor children through a will, thus securing their futures.

Aristotle's approach was essentially an early form of trust creation, reminiscent of Terence's narrative in "The Woman from Andros," where he proposed marriage between Nicanor and his daughter as a means to transfer his wealth. Pythias the Younger, being an *epiklêros*—or an heiress in the absence of a male heir—was at the center of a practice aimed at preserving family estates through strategic marriages. After Nicanor's death, she married Procleus, a reputed descendant of Spartan King Demaratus and a student of Theophrastus, Aristotle's esteemed pupil. Although Procleus's ultimate fate is unclear, Pythias's subsequent marriage to a physician, with whom she had a child named Aristotle, underscores the continuous efforts to secure a legal protector for her and her property. This series of marriages was not just about personal union but also about finding a suitable steward for her inheritance, illustrating the complexities of ancient inheritance practices and the lengths to which Aristotle went to ensure his daughter's protection and prosperity.

Protecting Minor Children

A common motivation behind the creation of trusts is the desire to safeguard the interests of minor children. This includes grandparents looking out for grandchildren, aunts assisting nieces, or parents caring for special needs children. Minors, by virtue of their age, lack the legal capacity and maturity to manage financial assets effectively.

Without a trust in place, the court typically appoints a guardian to oversee the child's finances. In some jurisdictions, the court may even establish a trust for this purpose. However, relying solely on court-appointed guardianships or trusts often has a significant limitation: they typically expire when the child reaches 18 years of age.

This age threshold can be problematic, as many children at 18 are not yet fully equipped to handle substantial financial responsibilities. Recognizing this, many opt to set up a trust that provides for the health, education, maintenance, and support (often referred to as a HEMS trust) of the child. Such trusts can extend well into the child's adult years, offering a more sustained form of financial support and guidance.

While it can be challenging to anticipate the exact needs of a young child in the future, trusts remain an invaluable tool for securing their financial well-being. They offer a structured, long-term approach to ensuring that the child's key needs are met, even when the original benefactors are no longer able to provide support directly. This foresight not only benefits the child but also gives peace of mind to those setting up the trust, knowing that their loved ones are cared for in the long term.

Analyzing the Impact of Windfalls on Different Age Groups

Joe, a seasoned attorney specializing in personal injury cases, tasked me with an intriguing project. His clients often received substantial settlements, particularly those involving disabled minor children. To safeguard these funds, Joe frequently resorted to setting up trusts or annuity contracts. He wanted concrete data to support a theory he had observed: the tendency of recipients, especially younger ones, to rapidly deplete their windfall.

Our research confirmed Joe's suspicions. We found that an average 18-year-old would typically exhaust a personal injury settlement within six months. Those in their mid-20s managed to preserve their funds for a few years, while by the age of 30, recipients generally treated their settlements no differently than their regular income.

The crux of our study was understanding why younger recipients tended to spend their windfalls quickly. We discovered that the root cause was often the erosion of their social structure. Initially, many attempted to save the money, but this frugality sometimes led to tensions and feelings of betrayal among their friends and family. This social rift left the recipients feeling isolated and led them to spend the money as a means of regaining social acceptance. The spending became a temporary salve for their emotional distress, but it often resulted in the complete depletion of their funds.

In contrast, older individuals tended to retain their windfalls longer, partly because their social circles were more stable and financially independent.

Joe termed this phenomenon "Dissipation." His study highlighted a critical insight: the importance of protecting young adults, particularly those between 18 and 25, from the temptation and potential pitfalls of handling large sums of money prematurely. By establishing a trust, a settlor can provide a structured and gradual distribution of funds, safeguarding the financial future of young beneficiaries and ensuring that the windfall serves its intended purpose of long-term support and stability.

The Importance of Establishing a Trust for Minor Children

There are several compelling reasons why setting up a trust for minor children is a prudent decision:

1. **Maturity Levels**: Minors often lack the maturity and experience to manage money effectively.
2. **Self-Support**: They are typically unable to support themselves financially.
3. **Social Structure**: Minors may focus their spending on maintaining their social network, which can lead to unwise financial decisions.
4. **Legal Limitations**: Children under the age of 18 cannot legally hold property, necessitating a guardian or trustee to manage their assets.
5. **Growth Through Struggle**: Experiencing financial limitations can be an important part of a child's development.

While both living trusts and testamentary trusts can be beneficial for minor children, a living trust has distinct advantages. It avoids probate, potentially shields assets from certain creditors, and offers more immediate and direct control over the assets.

Our legal system may recognize 18-year-olds as adults, but neuroscientific research suggests that brain development, particularly in areas related to decision-making and impulse control, continues into the mid-20s. This developmental fact underscores why a trust is valuable: it can provide financial oversight and gradual distribution of assets until a child reaches an age where they are better equipped to manage their inheritance responsibly.

In my experience, the age of 25 often marks a turning point in financial maturity. While there are exceptions, this age generally represents a stage when individuals are more capable of handling their financial affairs effectively.

Personal anecdotes and professional observations alike reveal that young adults often underestimate the cost of living independently. A well-managed trust can provide financial support while simultaneously teaching valuable life lessons about money management.

Moreover, the phenomenon of 'Dissipation' shows that young recipients of windfalls frequently spend a significant portion of their funds on non-essential or impulsive expenses, including bailing out friends. A trust can help mitigate this by ensuring that the funds are used for the child's actual benefit.

Finally, since minors cannot legally own property, creating a trust allows a trustee to manage the assets on their behalf, aligning with their best interests. This arrangement can eliminate the need for a guardianship, providing a more streamlined and effective way to manage a minor child's estate.

Therefore, establishing a trust for minor children is not just a financial decision but a thoughtful way to ensure their well-being and future stability.

Testamentary Trusts: Concerns and Considerations for Minor Children

While many attorneys advocate the use of testamentary trusts to protect minor children, there are significant concerns to consider. A testamentary trust is established within a will and has two main drawbacks:

1. **Probate Requirement**: Being part of a will, a testamentary trust must undergo probate. This process can be time-consuming and may incur additional costs.
2. **Vulnerability to Creditors**: The assets in a testamentary trust are subject to probate, making them potentially accessible to creditors. This is a crucial concern for young parents who may have considerable debt. Typically, life insurance proceeds earmarked for children's future are funneled into these trusts. If the estate is the named beneficiary, these proceeds are exposed to creditor claims, potentially leaving little to nothing for the children.

It's important to remember that the likelihood of both parents dying simultaneously is quite low. Not setting up a trust does not equate to being a bad parent, especially considering the financial burden of trust creation.

However, for single parents or those with significant assets or debts, having at least a testamentary trust is essential.

A living trust, though more expensive, is generally a better option for safeguarding minor children's interests. Unlike a testamentary trust, a living trust avoids the probate process and offers more direct control over assets, ensuring that they are used as intended and protected from creditors.

In summary, while testamentary trusts offer a level of protection for minor children, they come with notable limitations, particularly regarding probate and creditor exposure. For those who can afford it, a living trust provides a more comprehensive and efficient solution for protecting a child's inheritance.

A Lesson in Parenting and Estate Planning

One of my clients, demonstrating a blend of foresight and parenting acumen, approached me with a unique request. In November, she sought to establish two trusts, one for each of her adult children, specifically designed to benefit her grandchildren. She intended these trusts as a thoughtful Christmas gift for her children, laying a foundation for future generations.

However, after six months had elapsed, neither child had taken the necessary steps to set up their respective trusts. Concerned about the lack of progress, I reached out to her, ready to discuss the possibility of a refund. She requested patience and assured me she would handle the situation.

Remarkably, within just two days of our conversation, both of her children contacted me to schedule appointments. The method she employed to motivate them was both unconventional and effective. She had decided to leverage her estate plan as an incentive, threatening to leave her entire estate to the Catholic Church if her children failed to establish the trusts for their offspring.

This incident serves as a profound example of how estate planning can intersect with family dynamics and parenting strategies. It highlights the importance of not only preparing for the future financially but also engaging and motivating family members to take active roles in securing their own financial legacies. Her approach underscores the necessity of proactive involvement in estate planning, especially when it involves the well-being and future of subsequent generations.

Pet Trusts: Safeguarding Your Pets' Future

In recent times, the traditional allure of large families has diminished for many Americans. As someone with five children, I've seen firsthand the shift in family dynamics. Increasingly, people are choosing to have pets instead of, or in addition to, children. While minor children can face challenges due to inadequate estate planning, the consequences for pets can be even more dire, sometimes tragically resulting in their euthanasia.

One effective way to ensure the well-being of your pets after your passing is through a pet trust. A pet trust is established by allocating a specific sum of money to a trustee, who is then responsible for the care and maintenance of your pets. It's crucial, however, to carefully structure the trust to avoid potential conflicts of interest.

It is advisable not to leave the residual assets of the pet trust directly to the caregiver. Doing so could inadvertently incentivize the caregiver to prioritize financial gain over the welfare of the pets. Instead, consider designating the remaining trust assets to a charity or another individual after the pets have passed away. This structure helps ensure that the primary focus of the caregiver is the care and comfort of your pets, rather than the financial benefit they might receive.

In essence, a pet trust is not just a financial arrangement; it's a reflection of the love and care you have for your pets. It provides peace of mind, knowing that your furry companions will be well looked after in your absence. For pet owners, this can be an essential component of a comprehensive estate plan, ensuring that their beloved pets continue to receive the love and care they deserve, even when they can no longer provide it themselves.

12: Probate Avoidance

Mr. Lu, diagnosed with stage four pancreatic cancer, conveyed his situation during our initial consultation. In such moments, I've learned the importance of doing my job well as part of the grieving process. Offering condolences, ensuring efficient completion of necessary tasks, and facilitating my client's ability to move forward are paramount. 'I have no children, never been married,' he added.

I inquired, 'Do you work?' to gauge any financial concerns for his remaining time.

'I retired a week before the cancer diagnosis,' he replied. This conversation, particularly this statement, remains vivid in my memory, influencing my own family planning.

'What are your plans for your property?' I asked.

He expressed a desire to leave everything to his nephew, including a rental property in Florida. Owning property in multiple states, Mr. Lu faced potential probate complications in each.

'I can establish a trust to bypass probate, ensuring direct asset transfer to your nephew,' I suggested. He agreed without further concerns about his nephew's financial responsibility, marital status, or potential heirs.

Though Mr. Lu's reasons to create a trust were few, they were significant. He aimed to simplify the process for his nephew, avoiding the complexities of intestate probate.

Tragically, Mr. Lu passed away less than three weeks after finalizing the trust. His nephew, Mr. Weng, contacted me from Florida for guidance. I briefed him on trust administration, including trustee duties, trust registration, tax obligations, and asset transfer.

Confused, Mr. Weng remarked, 'I thought this would be simpler than probate?'

I clarified the more arduous probate process, involving executor applications, beneficiary notifications, hearings, bonds, and estate authority, all before managing the trust as previously described, and all replicated in Florida.

Understanding the intricacies of probate, Mr. Weng appreciated his uncle's foresight, allowing him the space to mourn appropriately.

Death Comes to All

A significant advantage of establishing a trust is avoiding the probate process and simplifying the administration of your estate. A common misconception is that having a will circumvents probate. In reality, probate exists to validate a will, or, in the absence of one, to determine the rightful heirs of an estate. When property is placed in a trust by the settlor during their lifetime, it bypasses the decedent's probate estate. Since the trust doesn't require validation like a will, the property within it is distributed according to the trust's terms, steering clear of probate court involvement.

The probate process can be lengthy and complex, especially when no estate plan is in place. Initially, it involves identifying an estate administrator and heirs. An application for heirship determination is filed in court to confirm both the administrator and the heirs. Additionally, the court appoints an attorney ad litem to represent unknown heirs. If all heirs consent, the administrator can act independently of court oversight. If not, a dependent administrator is necessary. Only after these steps can notice to creditors be given and an inventory of the estate be compiled. This entire procedure can be both costly and time-consuming. In contrast, a living trust circumvents these probate complexities.

Reasons to Opt for a Trust Over Probate:

1. **Increased Flexibility**: Trusts provide more leeway in how assets are transferred.
2. **Immediate Transfer**: Trusts eliminate delays in property transfer upon death.

3. **Cost Savings**: Avoidance of probate administration costs and court fees.
4. **Privacy**: Keeping the decedent's financial affairs confidential.
5. **Tax Protection**: Shielding the estate from various taxes.
6. **Ease of Validation**: Eliminating the need to legally prove a will's legitimacy.
7. **Creditor Protection**: Safeguarding assets from creditor claims.
8. **Reduced Contestability**: Lowering the risk of legal challenges to the estate.
9. **Simplicity**: Making the process more understandable and aligned with the settlor's intentions.

In summary, while probate can be an arduous and public process, a living trust offers a private, efficient, and flexible alternative for managing and distributing assets. This makes trusts an attractive option for those looking to streamline their estate planning and ensure their wishes are fulfilled without unnecessary legal hurdles or delays.

Probate Considerations in Estate Planning

While avoiding probate is often a key focus in estate planning, there are circumstances where undergoing probate might be advisable. In some cases, an attorney may recommend probate as the best course of action. This is particularly true when an objective, transparent process is needed for asset distribution, especially in situations where familial conflicts might arise. Probate courts provide a public, structured environment for resolving disputes related to property ownership rights.

Trusts are a common tool for bypassing probate. However, it's important to note that for a trust to control real estate, the property must be legally transferred to it, typically through a deed. A frequent oversight in estate planning, even with a trust in place, involves real estate. I recall a situation where I had to correct a colleague who had mistakenly assigned real property to a trust without deeding it. Fortunately, we resolved the issue by probating the will to transfer the property into the trust.

Strategies for Avoiding Probate Using Trusts

Creating a living trust doesn't automatically negate the need for probate. Estate planning attorneys often draft pour-over wills[21] to address this. The cornerstone of using a trust to avoid probate lies in ensuring the trust legally owns the relevant properties. This transfer of ownership can happen either during your lifetime or after your passing. A practical approach involves categorizing your assets into real and personal property and then meticulously listing them to verify their alignment with your trust. I use a client intake process that helps in identifying all assets and determining the necessary steps to incorporate them into the trust effectively.

---

[21] A pour-over will transfers assets to a living trust, or it requires the maker (the "Testator") to first create a trust and appoint a trustee to handle all or some of the maker's assets after death.

13: Creditor Protection Trusts

Approaching the end of his life, Brigham Young, the Mormon leader, had a vast family comprising 19 wives and 286 children, alongside an estate valued at over two and a half million dollars, equivalent to approximately 50 million dollars today. He designated his son, John W. Young, as the executor of his will, entrusting him with the significant responsibility of overseeing the welfare of his 285 siblings. For this monumental task, John was compensated with $10,000 and household furnishings. Brigham Young's will stipulated that the remainder of his estate was to be distributed among his 19 wives, with the residual assets to be divided among his children and any surplus directed towards charitable support for the poor. The will posed a logistical challenge in allocating the estate first to one group and then any residue to another.

Brigham Young's directive to his executor was unequivocal regarding his debts: "I have always paid my debts; damned be he that pays my debts." This statement raises a poignant question about prioritizing beneficiaries in estate planning: Should an estate's assets be directed towards settling debts with creditors or bequeathed to one's children? The dilemma of honoring debts versus providing for one's family is complex. While friends, family members, and employees might be considered as 'good' creditors worthy of repayment, the decision to bypass other creditors is highly personal. Consulting with an attorney is crucial to understand the implications and legal consequences of such decisions in estate planning.

The story of Ken Lay, the former CEO of Enron, and the protection of his assets following the Enron scandal and his subsequent death, is a notable example of asset protection strategies in action.

The Rise and Fall of Enron:

While Brigham Young was committed to fulfilling his financial obligations, not everyone has followed his standard. Ken Lay was the CEO of Enron Corporation, an energy company that became infamous for one of the most significant corporate frauds in history. In 2001, Enron filed for bankruptcy following revelations of widespread accounting fraud. This collapse led to significant legal troubles for Lay, including charges of fraud and conspiracy.

Despite the legal and financial turmoil, Lay employed several asset protection strategies to safeguard his personal assets:

1. **Homestead Protection in Texas:** Lay took advantage of Texas's homestead protection laws, one of the most generous in the United States. These laws protect a person's primary residence from most creditors, regardless of the home's value. Lay's primary residence in Houston, therefore, was shielded from claims by creditors.

2. **Other Assets:** It's reported that Lay also had other assets, including retirement accounts and possibly life insurance policies, which generally are afforded protection under federal and state laws. These assets are often shielded from creditors in bankruptcy and legal proceedings, helping to secure a financial safety net for the individual and their family.

Ken Lay's Death and Aftermath:

Lay passed away in 2006 from heart disease before sentencing could occur. Upon his death, several legal and financial outcomes ensued:

1. **Abatement of Criminal Charges:** Lay's death led to the abatement of his criminal charges. In the U.S. legal system, if a defendant dies before appeals are exhausted, their conviction can be vacated. As a result, Lay died legally innocent of the charges against him.

2. **Asset Transfer to Family:** Due to the asset protection strategies Lay had in place, and the legal principle of abatement, much of his wealth was insulated from creditors and legal claims. Consequently, these protected assets were able to pass on to his family.

3. **Protection from Civil Lawsuits:** Lay's death also impacted civil lawsuits against him. While certain claims against his estate could still

proceed, the protections he had in place for his homestead and other assets meant that a significant portion of his wealth remained shielded.

The case of Ken Lay and Enron illustrates how asset protection strategies can have a profound impact, even in the midst of significant legal and financial challenges. It demonstrates the effectiveness of homestead protections, the shielding of retirement accounts and life insurance, and the complexities of legal proceedings following an individual's death. This story serves as a reminder of the importance of understanding and utilizing asset protection strategies within the framework of the law.

Protecting assets from creditors is one of the primary purposes of creating a trust. It's true that under certain circumstances, a trust can protect against the claims of creditors; however, a trust cannot be created for the purpose of defrauding creditors. That is an illegal act in most states. Most states have enacted statutes like the Uniform Fraudulent Conveyance Act of 1918 or the Uniform Fraudulent Transfer Act of 1984. Within these statutes, trusts that transfer assets with the "intent to hinder, delay, or defraud any creditor..."[22] are restricted. The code also defines a fraudulent transfer in terms of the time when the transfer is made: "...a transfer is fraudulent as to a creditor whose claim arose before the transfer was made..."[23]

It is important to note that while creating a trust to avoid your own creditors might be illegal, you have no duty to another person's creditors. Many people worry that they are responsible for their parents' debts. This is not the case. Others fear that their children's inheritance will be subject to creditors. Thankfully, a spendthrift clause within a trust prohibits the

---

[22] Uniform Fraudulent Transfer Act section 4(a)
[23] Uniform Fraudulent Transfer Act section 5(a)

beneficiary from transferring his or her interest and prevents the beneficiary's creditors from taking the beneficiary's interest in the trust property. This clause is almost universal to all trusts because of its simple but powerful application.

Since protecting children from their creditors is an important benefit of trusts, many people would like to do that for themselves. We refer to these trusts as *asset protection trusts* or *self-settled spendthrift trusts*. To form one, a settlor creates an irrevocable trust with a spendthrift provision and names himself as the beneficiary. The Uniform Trust Code section 505 has provisions against this type of spendthrift provision. Since the United States has been so restrictive against these types of trust, other countries have picked up on this opportunity. *Offshore trusts* have sprung up in the Cook Islands, the Caymans, and Barbados to allow these types of trusts. These trusts are expensive but offer incredible asset protection because of local laws. In the United States, there are 17 states (Alaska, Delaware, Hawaii, Michigan, Mississippi, Missouri, Nevada, New Hampshire, Ohio, Oklahoma, Rhode Island, South Dakota, Tennessee, Utah, and West Virginia, Wyoming, and Virginia) that have significantly reduced their restrictions on self-settled spendthrift trusts. Nevada and South Dakota seem to be the most popular states at the moment.

While many jurisdictions have changed their laws to allow a settlor to create a trust to protect his or her assets from creditors, the general rule is you cannot create a trust to protect yourself from creditors. However, you can create a trust to protect your assets from going to your beneficiary's creditors.

Asset Protection Trusts: Balancing Family Dynamics and Financial Security

Jeff's story is a poignant example of the complex family dynamics often intertwined with estate planning. His mother, Emma, faced a dilemma: she wanted to ensure Jeff's welfare after her passing, yet she was concerned about his financial irresponsibility and outstanding debts.

Navigating the Challenges:

1. **Protecting the Home from Creditors:** Emma's primary concern was safeguarding her home from Jeff's creditors, particularly the IRS. The solution lay in creating a trust that would bypass probate, allowing her to control the property posthumously without giving Jeff outright ownership. This strategy would shield the asset from creditors.

2. **Spendthrift Trust Considerations:** To address Emma's worries about Jeff's spending habits, we discussed establishing a spendthrift trust. This type of trust restricts the beneficiary's access to funds, preventing reckless spending and protecting the assets from potential creditors, including the IRS.

3. **Selecting a Trustee:** The choice of a trustee is critical, especially when family tensions are involved. Emma initially considered her granddaughter, Ashley, despite the strained relationship between Ashley and her father, Jeff. Ultimately, she agreed to this, recognizing the importance of keeping decision-making within the family.

4. **Communicating the Plan:** Breaking the news to Jeff required tact and clarity. We explained that the estate would be divided equally between him and his brother, with the provision for Jeff to reside in Emma's house. By framing the trust as a protective measure against his creditors, Jeff understood and accepted the arrangement, with Ashley as the trustee.

Reflecting on the Outcome:

Despite initial challenges, Ashley and Jeff eventually reconciled, highlighting the evolving nature of family relationships. A spendthrift trust not only protected Jeff's inheritance but also played a role in mending their relationship.

Broader Implications:

A spendthrift trust is not just a financial tool; it's a means of safeguarding your children's future, even in complex family situations. It can protect their inheritance from external threats like creditors and divorces, offering peace of mind that their inheritance will be preserved for their benefit. In Emma's case, the trust served as a bridge, helping to rebuild the strained relationship between her son and granddaughter while securing her son's financial future.

Establishing a Creditor Protection Trust: Legal Considerations

Creating an asset protection trust is a viable option for safeguarding assets, but it requires careful planning and execution. This type of trust needs to be established in a state that legally permits creditor protection trusts. Setting up such a trust typically involves costs ranging from $10,000 to

$25,000, along with annual trustee fees starting from about $1,500. For those concerned about asset protection, consulting with an attorney specializing in this field is crucial, as trusts can offer significant protection. It's also worth noting that in some states, other forms of asset protection like annuities, life insurance, retirement accounts, and your primary residence may provide similar benefits.

Other Asset Protection Strategies

While creditor protection trusts offer robust asset security, they can be costly. For example, a firm I work with in Nevada charges $15,000 for establishing such a trust, plus an annual trustee fee of $2,500. Despite the expense, these trusts are often a worthwhile investment for affluent individuals.

Expanding on Asset Protection Strategies Across Different States

Asset protection strategies can significantly vary depending on state laws. Understanding how different states like Texas and Florida protect assets such as homesteads, retirement accounts, and insurance products is crucial. While creditor protection trusts are effective, they are not the only method of safeguarding assets. In many cases, more economical methods are available and sufficient.

Homestead Protection:

1. **Texas:** The Texas Constitution offers robust protection for homesteads. In Texas, a homestead is shielded from most creditors, making it one of the most effective asset protection tools in the state. Additionally, Texas

homestead laws may provide bankruptcy protection, though it's always advisable to consult with a bankruptcy attorney for specific guidance.

2. **Florida:** Similar to Texas, Florida provides strong homestead protection, exempting the primary residence from creditor claims, even in bankruptcy situations. This protection is part of why Florida is often considered a favorable state for asset protection.

Retirement Accounts:

1. **IRA and 401(k) Accounts:** Federal law offers protection for certain retirement accounts like 401(k)s, shielding them from creditors in bankruptcy. Individual Retirement Accounts (IRAs) also receive protection, but the limits may vary. These protections are in place as part of the government's initiative to encourage retirement savings.

2. **State Protections:** Some states offer additional protections for retirement accounts beyond federal provisions. It's important to understand your state's specific laws regarding these accounts.

Life Insurance and Annuities:

1. **General Protection:** Life insurance policies and annuities often have creditor protection elements, which can vary by state. These protections are designed to ensure that beneficiaries receive the benefits, not creditors.

2. **State-Specific Rules:** For example, in some states, life insurance cash values and annuity contracts are protected from creditors to a certain

extent. The degree of protection can depend on the relationship between the insured and the beneficiary.

Considering Alternatives to Trusts:

Before opting for a creditor protection trust, it's beneficial to explore other asset protection methods. Homestead laws, retirement account protections, and insurance product safeguards can provide adequate protection for many individuals. Trusts, while effective, can be more complex and expensive.

It's important to remember that asset protection strategies should be tailored to your specific situation and state laws. Consulting with an attorney to understand the best approaches for your circumstances is crucial. If a trust is suggested as the only option, it may be wise to seek a second opinion to ensure all potential strategies are considered.

14: Tax Planning Strategies

Mr. and Mrs. Dunham arrived in a 2006 Honda Civic, embodying the modesty of an 80-year-old couple from a simpler walk of life. Their attire and demeanor suggested unassuming means. Mr. Dunham presented me with his Charles Schwab portfolio, revealing investments exceeding $35 million, a staggering sum rarely seen in my practice.

"We need to revise our will," he declared.

He handed me a will from 1985, notably outdated and mentioning minor children. "Is this your only estate planning document?" I inquired.

"Yes, it's sufficient for us. Additional planning is unnecessary."

"Mr. Dunham, are you aware of the estate tax implications? The exemption caps at $5,430,000. Beyond that, taxes could reach 40%."

135

His expression indicated he had heard this before. "My wife and I together have nearly an $11 million exemption. You're likely trying to sell me an elaborate trust when a simple will suffices."

Despite an hour-long discussion, Mr. Dunham remained adamant. His frugality, evident in both his lifestyle and mindset, was a cornerstone of his wealth. No argument of mine swayed him. I faced a dilemma: Drafting a mere will could result in a substantial estate tax liability, potentially leading to legal actions against me from disgruntled heirs.

"Mr. Dunham, a basic will won't suffice. Your situation demands a more robust plan. Drafting a simple will exposes me to significant legal risks. It's prudent to assemble a team of specialists for your estate planning."

"What if I absolve you of liability?"

"That might mitigate legal consequences, but I'd still risk spending extensive time defending a basic service. Is that reasonable?"

Frustrated, Mr. Dunham stood up. "You lawyers are all the same, overcharging for mere paperwork."

They left, and though I harbored no resentment, I hoped no other attorney would acquiesce to his request.

The Estate & Gift Tax

Estate taxes are often considered a concern for those with substantial wealth. As of 2024, estates valued under $13.61 million are exempt from federal estate taxes (however, the exemption amount will be "sunset" to 7 million per person in 2026), though this threshold is subject to annual adjustments. The following chart illustrates the evolution of the exemption limit and top tax rate over the past century.

The idea of taxing estates is not new. The U.S. Congress, however, has struggled to maintain a consistent approach to estate and inheritance taxes, which have been a part of societies for millennia, primarily serving two purposes: funding wars and preventing wealth accumulation within a few families. Over time, various strategies have emerged to circumvent these taxes, such as gifting assets to heirs. To counteract this, the federal gift tax was introduced in 1924. With frequent legislative changes every few years, predicting estate tax liabilities can be a complex task, making trusts an essential tool in estate planning.

Another tax-avoidance strategy involves skipping generations in asset transfers, such as grandparents leaving assets directly to grandchildren. This action triggers the generation-skipping transfer tax, imposed to prevent avoidance of taxes due on transfers to the immediate next generation. Trusts, particularly dynasty trusts, are often used to manage assets across generations while minimizing tax liabilities.

Regarding the taxation of gifts, beneficiaries generally do not owe income taxes on received gifts, bequests, or inheritances, as outlined in I.R.C.

section 102(a). This includes transfers into trusts. However, beneficiaries might be liable for capital gains taxes on the appreciation of trust assets.

In addition to federal laws, some states impose their own estate and inheritance taxes, adding another layer of complexity to estate planning.

Trusts that Help Reduce Income and Capital Gains Taxes

 The following trusts are designed to help reduce income and capital gains taxes:

1. **Charitable Remainder Trust (CRT):** This trust allows you to receive a stream of income for a set period or for life, after which the remainder of the trust assets goes to a designated charity. It can provide an immediate income tax deduction for the charitable portion of the trust and can also help in deferring or reducing capital gains taxes.

2. **Charitable Lead Trust (CLT):** In a CLT, a charity receives income from the trust for a set period, and then the remaining assets pass on to your beneficiaries. This setup provides an income tax deduction for the value of the income interest given to the charity.

3. **Grantor Retained Annuity Trust (GRAT)**: This trust allows the grantor to receive a fixed annuity payment for a term of years, after which the remaining assets pass to the beneficiaries. The grantor pays income taxes on trust earnings, but the assets transferred to beneficiaries can avoid additional taxes.

4. **Intentionally Defective Grantor Trust (IDGT)**: The grantor continues to pay income taxes on the trust income, but the assets in the trust are removed from their estate. This can be beneficial if the trust's assets are expected to appreciate significantly.

5. **Irrevocable Life Insurance Trust (ILIT)**: While primarily used for estate tax purposes, an ILIT can also have income tax benefits. The life insurance proceeds can be free of income tax when paid to beneficiaries, and if the trust is structured properly, it can avoid generation-skipping transfer tax.

6. **Nongrantor Trust**: Unlike a grantor trust, a nongrantor trust pays its own income taxes. Under certain circumstances, this can be advantageous if the trust's income tax rate is lower than the grantor's rate.

7. **Complex Trust**: This type of trust has certain rights and powers which can accumulate income within the trust or distribute it to beneficiaries. Depending on the trust's and beneficiaries' tax situations, it can be used to optimize overall tax efficiency.

Each of these trusts serves specific purposes and can offer various income tax advantages under certain conditions. It's crucial to consult with a qualified tax advisor or estate planning attorney to determine the best approach for your individual situation, as trust law and taxation can be complex and vary depending on your location and circumstances.

Trust That Reduce Federal Estate and Gift Taxes

1. **Irrevocable Life Insurance Trust (ILIT)**: This trust is created to own your life insurance policy. The death benefit is not included in your estate, potentially reducing estate taxes. Gifts to the trust to pay premiums can qualify for the annual gift tax exclusion.

2. **Bypass Trust (also known as Credit Shelter Trust)**: Used by married couples to take full advantage of their federal estate tax exemptions. When the first spouse dies, assets up to the exemption limit are placed in the trust, reducing the taxable estate of the surviving spouse (this trust is not required by the IRS to preserve a spousal exemption limit).

3. **Qualified Personal Residence Trust (QPRT)**: Enables you to transfer your home to a trust while retaining the right to live there for a term of years. After the term, the home passes to your beneficiaries, potentially reducing gift and estate taxes.

4. **Grantor Retained Annuity Trust (GRAT)**: You transfer assets to this trust and receive a fixed annuity for a term. After the term, the remaining assets pass to your beneficiaries, often with reduced gift taxes due to the annuity payments you received.

5. **Charitable Lead Trust (CLT)**: This trust provides an income stream to a charity for a term, after which the remaining assets go to your beneficiaries. It can offer gift tax advantages on the assets passed to the beneficiaries.

6. **Charitable Remainder Trust (CRT)**: The reverse of a CLT, it provides you or other non-charitable beneficiaries with income for a term, with the

remaining assets going to a charity. It can result in a charitable deduction, reducing your taxable estate.

7. **Generation-Skipping Trust (GST)**: Allows assets to be passed directly to grandchildren or later generations, potentially avoiding the taxes that would apply if assets passed through each generation.

8. **Intentionally Defective Grantor Trust (IDGT)**: You transfer assets to the trust but retain certain powers, resulting in income tax responsibilities but removing the assets from your estate for estate tax purposes.

9. **Dynasty Trust**: Designed to last for multiple generations, this trust can help avoid estate taxes on assets as they pass through generations, within the limits of the generation-skipping transfer tax.

10. **Spousal Lifetime Access Trust (SLAT)**: One spouse creates this irrevocable trust for the benefit of the other spouse. It can remove assets from both spouses' estates while still providing financial support to the beneficiary spouse.

Each of these trusts is designed for specific scenarios and offers distinct advantages in reducing federal estate and gift taxes. Their effectiveness can vary based on individual circumstances, including the size and composition of your estate, your family structure, and your long-term financial goals. Consulting with an estate planning attorney or a tax advisor is crucial to tailor a strategy that aligns with your personal situation and complies with current laws and regulations.

Irrevocable Life Insurance Trust

An Irrevocable Life Insurance Trust, "ILIT", is irrevocable, of course, and the trust is both an owner and beneficiary of a life insurance policy.[24] An ILIT is usually set up for two reasons: (1) to place a large life insurance policy in a trust where it cannot be changed by the settlor or the beneficiaries and (2) to move a large sum of money outside of a taxable estate. Life insurance proceeds owned by an individual do not escape federal estate taxation.[25] However, the insurance proceeds owned by an ILIT both escape these taxes and can be controlled by the person who funds the trust.

Let's discuss the funding of an ILIT. A life insurance trust can be funded or unfunded at creation. A funded life insurance trust contains an income-producing asset to help pay premiums. Two issues arise from a funded ILIT: (1) a gift tax is imposed with the transfer of income producing assets to a trust, and (2) IRC 677(a)(3) states that a grantor is to be taxed on the trust income.

An unfunded life insurance trust avoids these two issues. Usually, the goal of an unfunded life insurance trust is for someone to pay the premiums with an annual gift under the gift exclusion amount. If cash exceeding the gift exclusion amount is used to pay these premiums, it will be subject to estate taxes. Funding a life insurance policy in an ILIT can be done with a loan from a bank, which is called premium- financing a life insurance policy.

---

[24] The Use of Life Insurance In Estate Planning: A Guide To Planning And Drafting, Jon J. Gallo, Fall 1999 Real Property, Probate and Trust Journal, American Bar Association.
[25] "Internal Revenue Code Section 2042(1)&(2)"

Premium Financing of a Life Insurance Policy

Everyone loves the fact that life insurance is protected from creditors, grows tax free, and gives the ability to borrow tax-free money. However, everyone hates to make the premium payment on his or her life insurance policy. It may surprise you to learn that financial institutions will give you a loan to pay the life insurance premiums on your behalf. They are willing to do this because life insurance policies can act as collateral for secured loans. Just like you can leverage your real estate assets, you can also leverage your life insurance policy. Since life insurance is a contract with a life insurance company, assuming you meet the qualifications for net worth and income, financial institutions consider premium financing of life insurance policies to be less risky than mortgage loans. In fact, some people never make one payment into their policy but die with a policy worth tens of millions of dollars.

Premium financing is a rich man's game that can only be offered to wealthy individuals. Most of my clients cannot do this because financial institutions will not loan them money unless they can afford to pay the interest on a multi-million-dollar loan.

Here is the basic idea[26]. Let's assume you take a loan of $500,000/year for the next seven years[27] from a bank to pay your life insurance premiums on a policy with a $10 million death benefit. In this situation, you must come up with the first-year interest payment of $20,000. Year two, you take another loan of $500,000 and pay another interest payment[28] of $40,000. Year three, another loan for $500,000 and another interest payment of $60,000. Hopefully, by year three, the policy is making enough money from being invested to pay the interest on the loan. You continue to take these loans for four more years. The policy is usually placed in an Index Life Insurance Policy, which moderates the policy holder's returns. This policy's return is usually dependent upon the S&P 500. If the market goes up 20% one year, the policy is capped at a lower rate, say 10%. If the market tanks -20%, some policies will protect against all losses and pay a 0% to 2% return. How does the insurance company do this? Simply put, they leverage your money and use complex hedging strategies to offset any losses. Don't worry, the major financial institutions will be just fine in this deal.

---

[26] This is a generic idea of how we structure these estate plan ideas and should not be used to determine how a policy will perform in the future. Interest rates differ with each policy, so some can be better than others. Also, we take an assumption on the growth of the policy based on historical data. Historical returns to not determine future returns.

[27] Why seven years? It has to do with the modified endowment contract rules set up by the IRS. Basically, the IRS has put limits on the amount of money that one can put into a policy. Why would they limit that? Remember that the cash value in life insurance grows tax-deferred, you can borrow against that value to get tax-free income, and you can potentially pass this money to your heirs with a tax-free death benefit. The IRS is very aware of just how good a tax sheltering instrument properly structured life insurance can be for you and your loved ones. The IRS just doesn't want you to abuse it or wealthy individuals to have a big tax loophole.

[28] Assuming the bank charges a 4% interest rate.

So, why is this so great? In 15 years, the bank will agree to loan you $306,000/year every year.[29] And yes, I said the bank. By year 20, the annual loan amount increases to $395,000. By year 24, the loan amount could increase to $455,000. If you wanted, by year 40, you could take a $1.25 million loan from the bank each year. Remember, you do not ever have to repay these loans in your lifetime. If 51-year-old individual lived 50 years, the policy would have almost a $100 million death benefit. Remember that all those loans will have to be repaid upon your death, but the remainder will go to your beneficiaries. In this example, the individual paid $60,000 out of pocket but accrued a death benefit for his family of $100 million, minus loan costs.

Based on these exorbitant numbers, you might be tempted to believe that this is a risk-free investment. After all, the bank pays for it, and you get all the benefits, right? Unfortunately, everything has risk. In this situation, the major risks are interest rates and market performance. The key to ensure that a premium financed life insurance policy stands the test of time is a good team that can manage the pitfalls of the future and structure a policy that works long-term.

Anyone with an Estate Tax Issue Should Have a Trust

Addressing estate tax concerns, whether they involve estate taxes, state taxes, local taxes, or generation-skipping transfer taxes, often necessitates the use of trusts as a strategic tool for burden reduction. This domain of

---

[29] This might be a little confusing. The loans you are now taking are from the bank out of your own policy. So, effectively, you are borrowing from yourself. You take loans from yourself to keep the policy in effect and avoid reporting income.

law demands extensive expertise in both tax law and trust law, and is typically handled by attorneys specializing in these areas.

When it comes to protecting substantial assets from estate tax liabilities, assembling a team of skilled professionals is not just advisable, it's a prudent investment. Yet, it's been observed that individuals with significant wealth frequently exhibit reluctance to allocate funds for estate planning. This hesitancy might stem from a lack of awareness regarding the substantial impact that effective estate planning can have on preserving their financial legacy.

Trust Tax Rates and Individual Tax Rates

In light of the Tax Cuts and Jobs Act (TCJA), the approach to trust planning for spouses, descendants, and other beneficiaries has undergone significant changes, particularly in terms of federal income tax liabilities. This transformation necessitates a deeper understanding and strategic planning to navigate these new challenges effectively.

The TCJA has notably widened the gap in tax treatments between trusts and individuals. Trusts now face more restrictive exemptions and higher tax rates compared to individuals. For instance, a trust with an income of $172,925 faces a substantially higher tax burden than a single individual or a married couple with the same income. This disparity extends to the taxation of capital gains and qualified dividends, where trusts are at a distinct disadvantage. An individual can earn a larger amount in qualified dividends annually without incurring federal income tax, unlike a trust.

Another significant aspect under the TCJA is the imposition of a 3.8% net investment income tax on trusts for amounts over $12,750, which is much lower than the threshold set for individuals. However, trusts do benefit from specific deductions like trustee fees and tax return preparation fees, which are not available to individuals.

Given these changes, estate planning professionals must carefully weigh the tax implications against the non-tax benefits of trusts, such as creditor protection and estate tax advantages. This becomes particularly crucial when considering distributions. While distributing all trust income to beneficiaries may reduce trust income tax rates, it could potentially conflict with the trust's intended purposes, especially in the case of minors or special needs beneficiaries.

Adaptable solutions have become key in this new landscape. Implementing a Section 678 withdrawal power, for instance, can shift the tax liability to beneficiaries, potentially lowering the overall tax burden. Trustee suspension powers also add a layer of flexibility, allowing for a balance between tax efficiency and other important trust objectives. For existing trusts, using state decanting laws or strategic distributions can facilitate the transition of assets into trusts with more favorable tax treatments.

This nuanced approach underscores the importance of harmonizing the objectives of asset protection and beneficiary welfare with the current tax landscape, emphasizing the need for strategic and informed planning in trust creation and management.

15: Beneficiary Protection

Diogenes Laertius gave us Plato's will which stipulated, "These things hath Plato left and bequeathed: The farm of Hephaestiades bounded, etc. It is forbidden to sell or alienate it; but it shall belong to my son Adimantes, who shall enjoy the sole proprietorship thereof…".

For some reason, Plato, the genius philosopher, felt like it was necessary to restrict his son from selling a farm. Why? We can only assume that if given full ownership over the land, Plato believed his son would have unwisely sold it. Sometimes, we need to protect our beneficiary from our beneficiary.

Trusts serve as essential tools not only for asset protection against external threats but also from the potentially detrimental actions of beneficiaries themselves. In my practice, I've observed that often the greatest risk to preserving wealth isn't external parties, but rather the beneficiaries. They may squander their inheritance due to drug addiction, reckless spending, poor financial management, gambling, or other harmful behaviors. Additionally, some individuals are easily swayed by the influence of family, friends, advisors, or fall prey to scams. Unplanned health issues can also significantly erode an inheritance. A trust effectively shields an inheritance from both internal and external elements that might otherwise deplete it.

In recent years, there has been a noticeable increase in opioid-related deaths among young adults. Consequently, incorporating provisions for drug addiction in estate planning has become increasingly crucial. A statement I once heard at a seminar resonates deeply: "the only thing that saves a heroin addict is bankruptcy." This highlights the importance of controlled financial access in such situations.

Moreover, those who inherit substantial wealth often attract unwanted attention, aimed at partaking in their fortune. A trust can delegate financial management to a more experienced individual, safeguarding the assets from these predatory approaches. I've often heard concerns from clients about trusting their child but not their child's spouse with an inheritance. Trusts can provide a protective barrier in these scenarios. Particularly for stay-at-home parents, who invest considerable trust in their working spouses, a trust is vital. During my tenure in family law, I frequently encountered stay-at-home parents, primarily mothers, who found themselves financially vulnerable following a divorce. Instances where a stay-at-home parent used their inheritance to pay off a spouse's debts, only to face divorce shortly after, were not uncommon.

The protection of disabled children requires careful planning. Contrary to popular belief, government assistance is typically limited to impoverished disabled individuals. Without proper planning, a disabled child may become a ward of the state. The Affordable Care Act has altered the landscape for supplemental needs trusts, as pre-existing conditions are now covered by regular health insurance, which can be funded by the trust. This offers more flexibility than traditional supplemental needs trusts. Special needs planning should be undertaken with an attorney specialized in this area.

Finally, for those children constantly chasing the next big, yet often unrealistic, financial breakthrough—the 'home-run-kids'—a trust can provide a safeguard. They might be prone to pursuing quick, lucrative schemes and can benefit from a trust structured to ensure long-term financial stability, like a retirement trust, to protect them throughout their pursuits.

Trust-Fund-Kids

Beneficiaries who rely solely on trust funds often face unique challenges. Overprotection through trusts can hinder the personal growth of these individuals, commonly referred to as 'trust-fund kids'. An overly restrictive trust can inadvertently shield them from life's struggles, which are essential for developing resilience and self-reliance. The delicate balance between providing financial security and encouraging personal development is crucial in trust creation.

Consider the case of Mary, a beneficiary I encountered. Her family's wealth, once valued at over $30 million, primarily stemmed from oil fields.

However, with diminishing returns from these assets, her monthly allowance had reduced to $5,000. Accustomed to a life of leisure, funded by her trust, Mary found herself ill-equipped to manage her finances or engage in meaningful employment. Her lifestyle of gambling and excess led her to exhaust her monthly funds quickly, plunging into debt.

Mary's situation reached a point where she contemplated suing the trustee for mismanagement, hoping to liquidate the family's mineral rights for immediate financial gain. However, a review of the trust revealed no wrongdoing by the trustee. I advised against the lawsuit, emphasizing the need for Mary to adapt to a more sustainable lifestyle within her means.

This story had a positive turn. Mary eventually embraced a significant lifestyle change. After filing for bankruptcy and undergoing rehabilitation, she returned to my office noticeably transformed and rejuvenated. Her story is not uncommon among trust-fund beneficiaries. It serves as a cautionary tale about the potential pitfalls of trusts that overly insulate beneficiaries from life's challenges, thereby impeding their personal growth and ability to manage adversity.

How Not To Create a Trust-Fund-Kid

Jamie's situation highlights the effectiveness of thoughtful trust planning and administration. The success of this trust can be attributed to several key factors that you might consider when advising clients on how to prevent creating a "trust-fund-kid" scenario:

1. **Purposeful Distribution Strategy**: The trust was designed with specific goals, such as funding education and supporting career choices. This

purpose-driven approach ensures that the trust benefits are used constructively, rather than fostering dependency.

2. **Selective Disbursement**: The trustees exercised discretion in distributing assets. They differentiated between needs and wants, providing funds for essential purposes while using the trust as a motivational tool for personal growth and financial independence.

3. **Education and Self-Sufficiency**: The beneficiaries were encouraged to pursue their own careers and develop self-sufficiency. This approach instills a sense of responsibility and work ethic, rather than creating a reliance on trust funds.

4. **Effective Trustee Selection**: The grandparents selected trustees who they trusted to honor their intentions and make wise decisions. A good trustee can be instrumental in guiding the trust according to its intended purpose and adapting to changing circumstances.

5. **Long-Term Vision**: The trust was established with a long-term perspective, considering the future needs and well-being of the beneficiaries, rather than just immediate financial support.

6. **Flexibility and Adaptability**: The trust was managed with a balance of firmness and flexibility, adapting to the changing needs and circumstances of the beneficiaries.

To replicate this success in other trust arrangements, consider these strategies:

- Clearly define the purpose of the trust and communicate this to both trustees and beneficiaries.
- Choose trustees who understand the family dynamics and can make decisions in line with the trust's objectives.
- Encourage beneficiaries to pursue education and career paths that lead to financial independence.
- Set up milestones or conditions for distributions that motivate beneficial behaviors, such as completing education or achieving certain personal goals.
- Regularly review and, if necessary, revise the trust terms to adapt to changing circumstances and needs.

By integrating these principles into trust planning, you can help clients create trusts that support their beneficiaries' growth and independence, rather than inadvertently fostering dependency.

Investing a Modest Amount to Secure a Significant Legacy

It's often startling to encounter individuals with substantial wealth who hesitate to invest a relatively modest sum in estate planning. This reluctance overlooks the crucial role of estate planning in ensuring that their wealth is not only transferred efficiently but also utilized prudently by their heirs. In a single consultation, a skilled estate planning attorney can develop a strategy that not only safeguards your beneficiaries but also prevents the formation of an irresponsible trust-fund beneficiary. Many clients are surprised to discover the simplicity of establishing an effective plan. The foundational aspect of this process involves addressing three key questions:

1. Whom do you trust to carry out your estate plan effectively?
2. To whom or where do you wish your assets to be transferred?
3. For what purposes should your assets be utilized?

While an estate planning attorney will certainly delve into more detailed discussions, these questions form the essence of your plan. Being able to provide clear answers to these questions sets the stage for your attorney to craft a comprehensive and tailored estate plan.

Life Stage Trust™

In my extensive experience guiding over 10,000 individuals in crafting their estate plans, a common question I encounter relates to how I manage my own family's estate planning. To address this, I developed the Life Stages Trust, a novel approach tailored to shepherd beneficiaries through the various pivotal phases of life. This trust, designed with the foresight of life's changing dynamics, provides structured support and oversight for my descendants at each key life stage: childhood, development, transformation, responsibility, and retirement. Each stage is thoughtfully crafted to meet the unique challenges and opportunities it presents.

Childhood Stage (18 and Younger)

Estate planning in childhood is primarily about ensuring that children are cared for in every aspect should the worst happen. It's crucial to appoint separate guardians for your child and their finances to prevent potential conflicts of interest. A key element is providing for psychological support for a child who loses their parents, guarding them against potential exploitation or neglect by the guardian.

Development Stage (19 to 25)

This stage marks the transition from adolescence to adulthood. It's a period where some might struggle with maturing, often referred to as the 'Peter Pan syndrome'. With the changing landscape of higher education, innovative approaches to development become essential. Inheritances at this stage can be vulnerable to rapid loss due to financial naivety, impulsive spending, and inadequate financial management.

Transformation Stage (26 to 35)

Focusing on career development or entrepreneurial ventures, this stage is a bedrock for future stability. The trust evolves into an income replacement trust during this phase, matching the beneficiary's earned income up to a certain limit and assisting with expenses like childcare, fostering both professional growth and family responsibilities.

Responsibility Stage (36 to 55)

This phase is often marked by heightened financial demands and limited personal time. The trust is structured to support essentials like retirement planning, family vacations, and activities that promote a well-rounded lifestyle, while consciously avoiding funding for luxury or extravagant expenses.

Retirement Stage (56 and Older)

As beneficiaries enter retirement, the trust shifts to a less restrictive model, focusing on health, education, maintenance, and overall support. The goal is to ensure a comfortable and dignified lifestyle in the retirement years. To further safeguard financial security, a provision in the trust designates 10% to 30% of the beneficiary's initial assets for retirement savings, providing a safety net even if other resources dwindle.

The Life Stages Trust is an embodiment of my philosophy in estate planning – it's about guiding and protecting beneficiaries through every walk of life, ensuring that the wealth serves as a tool for growth and stability, rather than a potential source of downfall.

16: Protect Your Privacy

"The Virtuoso," a comedy that debuted in 1676, revolves around two young men enamored with the nieces of the eccentric Sir Nicholas Gimcrack. In a memorable scene, Sir Nicholas's will is proclaimed, stating, "my eldest son John, having expressed disdain for his little sister, whom I preserve in Spirits of Wine, and shown undutiful behavior towards me in numerous respects, is hereby disinherited and excluded from any portion of my personal estate, receiving instead a mere cockle-shell." Although the play is comedic, it highlights the enduring impact of disowning a child through a will. More than three centuries on, the extreme disinheritance executed by Nicholas Gimcrack still draws laughter for its sheer absurdity. It's essential to bear in mind that probated wills can endure longer than any other legacy you leave behind. The contents of your will may serve as a reflection of your character and intentions, impacting how you are remembered throughout history.

The advent of the internet and social media has significantly challenged the concept of privacy, particularly regarding personal information. This issue extends beyond life, as the probate process upon one's death turns private matters into public records. Wills, once probated, become accessible, exposing family decisions to public scrutiny. Disinheriting a child, for instance, can become public knowledge, inviting unwanted attention and questions.

Probate records have been a rich source for historical and genealogical research. They often provide comprehensive details, including the names of an individual's children. In my practice, I include all children, even those who were adopted away, to ensure any inheritance rights are addressed at the will's creation. Without a will, probate records still identify heirs, which can be problematic if certain familial relationships were meant to be private.

My own exploration into genealogy led to surprising discoveries, such as a child born shortly after my grandparents' marriage. A friend shared a similar experience regarding his grandfather, a prominent figure who advocated premarital abstinence. The posthumous revelation of his youthful indiscretion through a court proceedings was a shock to the family, highlighting the potential for embarrassment when private histories are unearthed.

Privacy concerns also extend to asset protection in legal contexts. As a new attorney, I learned about programs used to assess an individual's asset profile for litigation purposes. Wealthy individuals often transfer assets out of their name to avoid being targeted in lawsuits. Conversely, finding no assets can influence legal strategy, like requiring larger retainers or accepting cases on a contingency fee basis.

The privacy aspect of trusts is another complex issue. While a trust's name, like "123 Living Trust," might obscure ownership details, property listings must include the trustee's name. Therefore, a record stating "[your name], trustee of the 123 Living Trust" can reveal ownership information. Choosing a trustee for your trust requires careful consideration to maintain privacy.

Publicly recorded probate cases exemplify these privacy concerns. For instance, in Mr. Johnson's case, the probate record disclosed details about his family, reasons for disinheritance, the executor, and the distribution of his assets. This level of detail, while valuable for legal and historical research, can be a significant invasion of privacy for the family involved.

Example of A Public Recorded Probate Case

Applicant	Johnson, Bobby Ray
Deceased	Johnson, Billy Ray

	OTHER EVENTS AND HEARINGS
08/02/2010	Citation
	RETURNED 8-9-2010
08/02/2010	Last Will & Testament
	COPY ONLY
08/02/2010	Application for Letters Testamentary (OCA)
08/23/2010	Probate Hearing (2:15 PM) (Judicial Officer Copeland, Weldon S)
	prove up
08/23/2010	Proof Handwriting & Signature
08/23/2010	Proof
	BY SUBSCRIBING WITNESS
08/23/2010	Proof of Death
08/23/2010	Order Admit Letters Testamentary & Issue Letters
08/23/2010	Oath
09/20/2010	Inventory or Affidavit in Lieu of Inventory (OCA)
09/21/2010	Auditors Approval Inventory & Appr
09/23/2010	Order Approve Inventory

Embarrassing Family History

My great-great-great-great-uncle John Willingham left the following will behind upon his death:

THE LAST WILL AND TESTAMENT OF JOHN WILLINGHAM OF LUNENBURG CO., VIRGINIA

In the Name of God Amen, I, John Willingham of the County of Lunenburg and parish of Cumberland, being sick and weak and only considering the uncertainty of human life, do make and ordain this my last Will and Testament. First and principally, I commit my Soul into the hands of my blessed Maker, trusting in his Mercies and in the Mercies of my dear Redeemer for the Remission of all my sins, desiring my Body may be decently enter'd at the discretion of my Executrix, hereinafter Named, and as to my Estate that it has pleased God to bless me withall, after all my just Debts are punctually paid I Give and Dispose of it in the following manner:

Item I Give and bequeath to my son Thomas one shilling sterling

Item II Give and bequeath to my son John one shilling sterling

Item III Give and bequeath to my daughter Christian my Negro boy Peter (I having already given my two sons what I desired for them)

Item IV Give and bequeath to my son Gerrald my Negro boy Jamey, one feather bed and furniture, two cows and calves, two sows and pigs, one mare and the land and plantation whereon I now live, and also ninety acres of land joining aforesaid plantation to him and his heirs and assigns forever. Desiring my beloved wife have possession of the said land during her widowhood or life. And as to the residue remainder of my estate be it of what nature soever it will, I lend it to my beloved wife during her widowhood or life and then do give and bequeath it to be equally divided between my two daughters Viz. Amey and Betty, unless my beloved wife should think fit to give proportion, and I do appoint and ordain my beloved wife Mary my whole and sole executrix of this my last will and testament, making void and null all other wills by me made here and do acknowledge this only to be my last will and testament. In witness whereof I have hereunto set my hand and seal this 2nd day of February 1750.

John Willingham, LS

Reaching the end of the document, I felt a profound shock. There's an internal conflict knowing that someone in my ancestral line once claimed ownership over other human beings. It's perhaps the first time I've experienced a sense of shame associated with my last name. I've always held my surname in high esteem; it embodies strength, and every Willingham I've known, including my father, his father, and my grandmother, has been an exemplary individual. I understand that the past operated under vastly different norms, perspectives, and circumstances. Yet, I find myself grappling with how to reconcile the loving family I know with this aspect of our history.

The idea that human beings were bequeathed as property is jarring to any contemporary reader. My great-uncle's legacy is indelibly marred by his role as a slaveholder. Discovering his casual references to owning slaves has irrevocably altered my perception of him. This revelation is likely to have a similar impact on anyone who learns of it, casting a long shadow over his reputation.

Avoid Embarrassment

It might seem unlikely that any stipulation in your will could be perceived negatively, but societal norms and perspectives shift significantly over time. For instance, consider that just two decades ago, it was not uncommon for parents to disinherit a child based on their sexual orientation. This practice, once relatively widespread, is now largely viewed as discriminatory and unacceptable. Such an evolution in societal attitudes highlights how what is deemed acceptable now may be judged differently in the future.

Given these shifting societal norms, the argument for maintaining privacy in estate planning becomes compelling. Opting for a trust over a will can offer this discretion. If you find yourself in a situation where you decide to disinherit a child, for reasons personal to your family dynamics, it's advisable to handle this matter with the utmost privacy. A trust allows you to keep such decisions within the family, away from public scrutiny, thus preserving family dignity and minimizing potential conflicts or judgments from outside the family unit.

17: Multi-Generational Planning

President James Polk, who was also a lawyer, took the initiative to draft his own will. He harbored a strong wish for his homestead to remain within his family line, ensuring it would never be owned by outsiders. Polk envisioned that the most deserving among his descendants would inhabit the property across generations. His will stipulated that a resident tenant should maintain the homestead in perpetuity. However, Polk's heirs contested this provision, initiating a legal challenge on the basis that it violated Tennessee's constitutional prohibition against perpetuities. Ultimately, the court sided with the heirs, declaring Polk's will invalid in this respect. This case underscores the complexity, even for lawyers, of multi-generational estate planning.

In my first book, I outlined a strategy for leaving a substantial inheritance, potentially up to a billion dollars, to one's heirs. The concept is straightforward but requires time and prudent investment. It's important to acknowledge, however, that there are no absolute guarantees in finance. Assuming global stability, the potential for such wealth accumulation over several centuries exists.

The 'rule of 72' is a key principle in understanding investment growth. By dividing 72 by the annual percentage return, you can estimate the number of years it will take for an investment to double. For example, a 7% annual return would mean an investment doubles roughly every ten years.

Rule of 72 Example

	Start With	Add 7%	End With
Year One	$10,000.00	$ 700.00	$ 10,700.00
Year Two	$10,700.00	$ 749.00	$ 11,449.00
Year Three	$11,449.00	$ 801.43	$ 12,250.43
Year Four	$12,250.43	$ 857.53	$ 13,107.96
Year Five	$13,107.96	$ 917.56	$ 14,025.52
Year Six	$14,025.52	$ 981.79	$ 15,007.30
Year Seven	$15,007.30	$ 1,050.51	$ 16,057.81
Year Eigth	$16,057.81	$ 1,124.05	$ 17,181.86
Year Nine	$17,181.86	$ 1,202.73	$ 18,384.59
Year Ten	$18,384.59	$ 1,286.92	$ 19,671.51

Consider a $1 million investment in a fee-free trust with a 7% nominal return. To reach a billion dollars, this amount needs to double ten times, requiring just over 100 years. With typical 1% annual fees, the timeline extends to around 120 years. For instance, if you start in 2062, the distribution would commence around 2182, likely benefiting your distant descendants. It's also crucial to factor in inflation when calculating real returns. The S&P 500 has averaged a 10% growth over the last century, but with an average inflation rate of just over 3%, the real return is closer to 7%.

A dynasty trust offers a mechanism for multi-generational wealth transfer. Historically, the rule against perpetuities, originating from the Duke of Norfolk's case in 1682, restricted long-term property control to prevent perpetual family ownership. However, modern reforms in over twenty states have either abolished or significantly altered this rule for trusts, paving the way for dynasty trusts. These trusts, limited only by the settlor's creativity, can enable extensive multi-generational estate planning, allowing families to preserve and grow their wealth over an indefinite period.

The Rothschild Family

While some tales about the Rothschild family veer into the realm of conspiracy, the true story of Mayer Amschel Rothschild's creation of a remarkable family dynasty is undeniable. Born in 1710, Mayer Amschel Rothschild began as a moneychanger and laid the foundation for a financial empire. He established five key financial centers in Paris, Frankfurt, Vienna, London, and Naples, each overseen by one of his sons[30]. His acumen in international financing enabled him to navigate through

---

[30] Pohl, Manfred (2005), "Rothschild, Mayer Amschel", *Neue Deutsche Biographie (NDB)* (in German), **22**, Berlin: Duncker & Humblot, pp. 131–133

tumultuous periods when local economies faltered. Mayer's strategy of keeping banking operations within the family and forging strategic marriages, including those with royalty, was pivotal in maintaining control over their financial institution.

Mayer's dynasty-building efforts were so effective that parts of his empire endured through major historical upheavals including the French Revolutionary War, the Napoleonic War, the Italian Wars of Independence, and both World Wars. His sons, Amschel Mayer, Salomon Mayer, Nathan Mayer, Calmann Mayer, and Jakob Mayer Rothschild, successfully perpetuated their father's legacy. Mayer Amschel Rothschild stands as a paragon of multi-generational estate planning.

As Paul Johnson notes, "[T]he Rothschilds are elusive. There is no book about them that is both revealing and accurate. Libraries of nonsense have been written about them...[31]." This book may not unravel all mysteries surrounding this unique family, but it aims to explore how Mayer Amschel Rothschild constructed such a lasting dynasty. His approach involved:

1. Setting high expectations for his children.
2. Articulating a clear and compelling legacy vision.
3. Convincing his children to uphold and continue this legacy.
4. Demanding accountability and results from those in leadership positions.
5. Minimizing risks through strategic diversification.
6. Instilling core principles and values in his children.
7. Planning with a vision that spanned multiple generations.

---

[31] Paul Johnson, *A History of the Jews*, p.317.

Not everyone is inclined to dedicate their life to crafting a multi-generational estate plan, but there are valuable lessons to be learned from the strategic and forward-thinking approach of Mayer Amschel Rothschild.

Snowball Trust Mechanism

The Snowball Trust Mechanism is an innovative estate planning tool designed to perpetuate wealth across generations, ensuring a lasting legacy. The concept behind a snowball mechanism in your trust is to perpetuate the legacy of property from one generation to the next. This is achieved by using a portion of the inheritance to purchase life insurance policies on the lives of beneficiaries upon the settlor's death, thereby ensuring that the subsequent generation benefits from this structured financial foresight.

Consider this hypothetical story of how the concept works. James Anderson, a local construction business owner, sought to ensure the long-term prosperity of his descendants. With the help of his attorney, Taylor, James established a Snowball Trust Mechanism within his estate plan. This innovative strategy was designed to use a portion of each child's inheritance to purchase life insurance policies upon James's death, with the proceeds aimed at benefiting future generations of the Anderson family.

After James passed away, the trust mechanism was activated, subtly laying the foundation for a generational legacy. His children, Elizabeth, Michael, and Sarah, each pursued their passions, contributing to the community's growth in education, sustainable construction, and arts. The Snowball Trust was securing their children's future through life insurance policies funded by their inheritances.

As years unfolded, the Snowball Trust's impact became increasingly evident. When Elizabeth unexpectedly passed, the trust's life insurance policy on her life paid out, injecting funds back into the trust. These funds were then used to purchase new policies for her grandchildren, ensuring the continuity of James's vision across generations. This cycle of foresight and planning facilitated not just financial security but also instilled a sense of stewardship and responsibility within the Anderson family.

Over decades, the Snowball Trust mechanism transformed James Anderson's vision into a tangible legacy, supporting his family through life's unpredictabilities and empowering them to contribute meaningfully to their community's prosperity. The trust not only ensured the financial well-being of the Anderson descendants but also perpetuated a legacy of community engagement and personal fulfillment, demonstrating the profound impact of thoughtful estate planning.

The Snowball Trust Mechanism represents a forward-thinking approach to estate planning, emphasizing long-term wealth accumulation and distribution across generations. It embodies a strategic use of life insurance policies to create a lasting financial legacy, ensuring that each generation builds upon the foundation laid by its predecessors, akin to a snowball effect: continuously growing and benefiting future descendants.

Find Out Your Own Multi-Generational Story and How You Can Add to It.

An interesting experiment is to go online and discover your genealogy. By lining up dates and trying to fill in the gaps, you can start to paint a picture of the lives of your ancestors. The more in-depth you get, the more you start to realize that some ancestors further the family line and build a foundation that sustains multiple generations. Others make horrible decisions that devastate the family for decades. If you take the time to plan out your own empire, you can help ensure that hundreds of years from now, the family won't see you as the weak link.

18: Professional Management

For a long time, I was skeptical about appointing financial institutions as trustees, mainly due to the frequent complaints I heard from beneficiaries about the high fees charged by these entities. However, my perspective has shifted over the years, as I've observed the execution of trusts post-mortem. The professional management and distribution of trust assets by financial institutions often justify the associated costs.

In certain states, a trust can be terminated against the settlor's wishes if all beneficiaries and the trustee agree, and the settlor has passed. Unfortunately, I have seen instances where trustees and beneficiaries have liquidated trusts in violation of state laws. Often, this is driven by beneficiaries desiring to use the trust funds for frivolous or questionable purposes. A professional trustee can be instrumental in preventing such mismanagement.

Nevertheless, since financial institutions are profit-driven, it's crucial to impose checks and balances on them, similar to those you would on a personal trustee. If appointing a financial institution as a trustee, it's wise to include provisions allowing beneficiaries or a trust protector to change the trustee if necessary. It's advisable to opt for a large, stable institution, as the 2008 financial crisis exemplified the vulnerability of even major firms like Lehman Brothers, Merrill Lynch, AIG, and others.

Most individual trustees lack financial expertise. In cases of mismanagement, a trustee might face legal liability for any resultant losses. This raises a significant question when considering a family member as a trustee: would you be able to take legal action against a relative if necessary? And even if you did, they might not have the assets to cover the losses. A corporate trustee, on the other hand, eliminates these concerns. They are detached from emotional decision-making and are versed in the principles of the Uniform Prudent Investor Act (UPIA).

Ultimately, most trusts drafted by attorneys stipulate that the trustee must enlist the services of a financial institution for asset management, due to the complexities of complying with the UPIA. A common requirement is that the chosen institution should manage a minimum of $100 million. This provision aims to ensure that the trust's assets are managed by a reputable and capable entity, rather than a lesser-known or less reliable firm.

Navigating Trusts and Medicaid Eligibility

The complexities of Medicaid eligibility can be daunting, as Mrs. Jenkins discovered during her mother's application process. After eight months and two rejections, frustration was high. Continuous communication with Medicaid provided different explanations each time, leading to an appeal.

When Medicaid's file finally arrived, it revealed a critical detail: the client was deemed to have excess assets. Despite numerous calls to Medicaid, this issue was never directly addressed. Mrs. Jenkins' mother's assets appeared to be below the eligibility threshold upon initial review. However, it emerged that Mrs. Jenkins, acting as trustee, had opened two qualified income trust (QIT) accounts. For Medicaid eligibility, a person must have less than $2,000 in countable assets at the start of each month. The combined total in these two accounts was slightly over this limit.

Upon contacting Mrs. Jenkins about the additional QIT account, it became clear there was a misunderstanding. Despite instructions to allocate most of the trust assets to the nursing home, keeping only a nominal amount for personal expenses, Mrs. Jenkins had retained extra funds in the trust for unforeseen needs.

This oversight had significant consequences. Each month, the total assets exceeded the Medicaid limit, leading to disqualification. The accumulated cost to the nursing home, now over $70,000, was ineligible for Medicaid reimbursement. Mrs. Jenkins' realization of the error highlighted the critical importance of precise asset management in qualifying for Medicaid. This situation underscores the challenges and intricacies involved in trust management and the necessity of adhering strictly to Medicaid's asset guidelines.

Opting for a Professional Trustee

Serving as a trustee often presents significant challenges. In many cases, appointing a family member, such as a child, to this role may not be the most prudent decision. Opting for a professional or corporate trustee, who possesses expertise in trust management, can greatly influence the trust's success. These institutions offer several advantages in trust administration.

Firstly, corporate trustees can pool resources from multiple trusts into one larger fund. This consolidation can lead to reduced costs, enhanced investment diversification, and access to more sophisticated asset management. These benefits are particularly valuable in the complex landscape of financial investments.

Moreover, from a legal perspective, the choice of a corporate trustee adds a layer of security. In situations where legal action becomes necessary, an attorney can confidently pursue a claim against a financial institution, with a reasonable expectation of recovery. This assurance is a significant consideration, particularly for those within the legal profession who understand the intricacies of trust litigation.

In summary, while the personal touch of a family trustee has its merits, the advantages of a corporate trustee - in terms of investment management, cost efficiency, and legal security - often make it a superior choice for trust administration.

The Rise of AI Fraud

In the bustling financial hub of Hong Kong, a reputable firm faced a staggering loss of 25 million dollars due to an intricately orchestrated fraud involving artificial intelligence. This incident unfolded when the Chief Financial Officer (CFO) received a request for a video chat from someone he believed to be the Chief Executive Officer (CEO) of the firm. The interaction was shockingly realistic, with the CEO's voice and appearance mimicking perfection, thanks to advanced AI-generated deepfake technology.

The so-called CEO urgently instructed the CFO to initiate a transfer of 25 million dollars to a specified account as part of a confidential and time-sensitive acquisition. Trusting the authenticity of the interaction, the CFO complied, only to discover later that the video chat was a fabrication engineered by fraudsters. This sophisticated deception not only resulted in a substantial financial loss but also exposed the vulnerabilities firms face in the digital age.

This cautionary tale serves as a stark reminder of the potential risks elderly individuals may encounter, particularly as AI technologies become more sophisticated. Elderly people, often perceived as less technologically savvy, are at a heightened risk of being targeted by scammers using AI to impersonate trusted individuals or authorities. The emotional and cognitive vulnerabilities that can accompany aging make them prime targets for such elaborate schemes, potentially leading to significant financial losses or the unauthorized transfer of assets.

To mitigate these risks, establishing a professionally managed trust emerges as a critical protective strategy. A trust can serve as a robust safeguard for an individual's assets, ensuring that they are managed and distributed according to the precise terms laid out in the trust agreement. Here's how a professionally managed trust can offer protection against AI-driven fraud and other scams:

1. Professional Oversight: A trust is managed by a trustee, typically a professional with expertise in finance, law, and asset management. This level of professional oversight means that any unusual or suspicious requests for asset transfer would be subjected to rigorous scrutiny, verification, and compliance with the trust's terms, significantly reducing the likelihood of fraud.

2. Defined Protocols for Transactions: Trusts often have clearly defined protocols for how transactions are to be executed, including multiple layers of verification for any substantial financial movements. This can prevent unauthorized access or transfers, as seen in the Hong Kong firm's case, by ensuring that any significant action requires more than just an instruction received via digital communication.

3. Legal Protection and Clarity: Trusts provide a legal framework that spells out the intentions of the settlor (the person who creates the trust) with clarity. This means that assets are managed and distributed in line with the settlor's wishes, providing a legal barrier against attempts to misappropriate assets through deception or coercion.

4. Education and Support for Beneficiaries: Trustees can also play a crucial role in educating and supporting beneficiaries, including elderly individuals, about potential scams and the importance of verifying information. This proactive approach can build awareness and resilience against fraud attempts.

While the advent of AI poses new challenges in asset protection, especially for vulnerable populations like the elderly, establishing a professionally managed trust offers a comprehensive defense mechanism. It not only provides a structured and secure way to manage assets but also incorporates checks and balances that are vital in the face of evolving technological threats. As we navigate this new digital frontier, the principles of caution, verification, and professional management remain our best defense against the sophisticated scams of the modern age.

19: Safeguarding Against Your Future Self

The tale of Jack's father is a heart-wrenching example of how the elderly can fall victim to online exploitation, leading to significant financial loss. Grieving the death of his wife, Jack's 70-year-old father sought companionship on an internet dating site, where he connected with a seemingly young, foreign woman. This relationship quickly escalated, with his father sending her ten thousand dollars for living expenses, followed by substantial amounts for building a home in Australia.

The family grew concerned about his mental state as he planned to relocate, but their efforts to have him declared incapacitated were unsuccessful. It was only after his death that the true extent of the deception was uncovered: the father had transferred his entire estate to this woman. Investigations revealed that the images he received were from a well-known porn star, indicating a sophisticated catfishing scheme.

Jack's inquiry about recovering the lost funds highlighted the grim reality of the situation. Unless the perpetrator could be located and apprehended in Australia, chances of retrieving the money were slim. This situation is a stark reminder of the vulnerabilities elderly individuals face, particularly between the ages of 75 and 100, when mental capacities can decline significantly. It underscores the need for vigilance and protective measures to safeguard the financial well-being of the elderly from such predatory practices.

Cognitive Decline

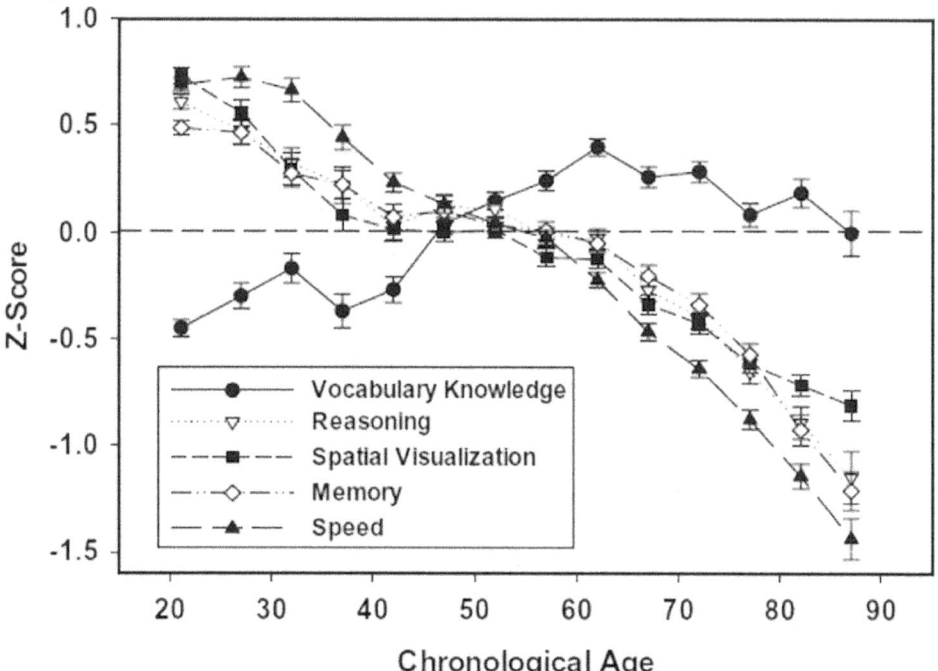

A commonly overlooked aspect of aging is the potential decline in mental capacity to manage financial affairs. As an attorney, I have encountered numerous instances where individuals, often in their later years, have made regrettable financial decisions. These include, but are not limited to, giving away substantial assets to unverified caregivers or salespeople, making disproportionately large financial contributions for minor family needs, and agreeing to financially burdensome commitments for acquaintances.

To safeguard against such scenarios, a family living trust can be a crucial tool. It can be structured to delegate the management of your assets to a trustee in the event of your mental incapacity. It is standard practice for trust management to transition to a successor trustee should the original trustee become mentally incapable. This allows for efficient and timely intervention to protect the settlor's assets.

In contrast, without a trust in place, there are significant risks. Should you become incapacitated without having a power of attorney or a trust, your family would be compelled to pursue legal guardianship over your estate. The process to legally determine mental capacity is not only prolonged but also fraught with difficulties. Judges often hesitate to declare someone incapacitated due to the severe loss of legal rights it entails, including the right to vote.

An illustrative example is a case involving a former Harvard professor who believed her rights were being infringed upon. She had been assigned a court-appointed attorney due to threats she had made against others, yet a judge had not deemed her mentally incapable, even refusing to revoke her legal right to own a firearm. When I declined to take her case due to these complexities, her threatening response further evidenced her unstable state.

This situation highlights that relying on a legal determination of mental incapacity can be uncertain and unreliable. Therefore, establishing a trust offers a more secure and direct means of ensuring your financial affairs are managed responsibly should you lose the ability to do so yourself.

Addressing Age-Related Decline in Mental Capacity

It's important to recognize that mental capacity can diminish with age. Research indicates that humans may start experiencing a gradual decline in mental capacity from around the age of 25. Although this decline is often subtle and initially offset by increasing life experience, it becomes more noticeable and impactful in later years. A study by the Boston University Public Health Department provides a compelling illustration of this decline, particularly after the age of 74. This is a crucial consideration for those considering appointing elderly parents as trustees or executors, as their ability to effectively manage such responsibilities may be compromised.

The concept of change and identity over time can be pondered through the lens of the Ship of Theseus, a thought experiment from Greek mythology. The ship, maintained as a memorial, underwent gradual replacement of its parts, leading to philosophical debates about its identity. Similarly, the human body undergoes significant cellular change over time. While we may feel a sense of continuity day-to-day, the cumulative changes can be substantial. This is particularly relevant in the context of aging loved ones, whose cognitive abilities might alter significantly over the years.

Given these considerations, setting up a revocable living trust can be a prudent measure. Such a trust allows you to safeguard your interests against potential future declines in mental capacity. Careful structuring of your trust to accommodate these changes is not just beneficial; it's a wise investment in your future well-being and peace of mind.

20: Appoint Your Own Judge

Amy was adamant. "I want him removed as trustee," she said, her voice firm. She was referring to her brother, Brandon. "I read the trust documents, and they state you, as the trust protector, have the authority to remove him."

I needed to tread carefully. I had the power indeed, but it was a responsibility entrusted to me by their mother, to be used judiciously. "That's true, Amy, but your mother intended that power for serious circumstances. What's the issue with Brandon?"

"He's not communicating with me, and he's not taking action," Amy complained.

"What kind of communication are you expecting? What actions do you want him to take?" I inquired, seeking clarity. Amy's grievances didn't yet suggest any gross misconduct on Brandon's part.

"I need a weekly update via email. And he needs to sell our property and distribute my share. I'm financially struggling!" Amy's frustration was evident.

After promising to return her call shortly, I contacted Brandon to discuss Amy's concerns. He was adamant against sending weekly updates and equally resistant to selling the property immediately. The conversation revealed underlying tensions, making the situation complex. I called Amy back to explain that legally, weekly updates weren't mandatory, though she could request an accounting. I also informed her that removal of a trustee required a violation of the trust terms, which hadn't occurred.

The situation escalated over the next few days, with legal counsel now involved on both sides. The conflict had spiraled, costing both Amy and Brandon over $3,000 in attorney fees – a far cry from their mother's intentions. I decided to reach out to Brandon's attorney, Mr. Evans.

"Mr. Evans, Taylor Willingham here. I'm calling about the ongoing dispute. Is there a chance we can find a resolution?" Our conversation, however, circled without nearing any solution.

Eventually, I pointed out a critical section in the trust documents. "Mr. Evans, could you refer to Article VI, Section E5? It grants me the authority to remove the trustee. Amy is next in line. Her demands for regular updates and the sale of the property seem reasonable to me. If Brandon remains uncooperative, I'll have no choice but to appoint Amy as trustee. He has a week to reconsider his stance."

Within two days, a breakthrough occurred. Brandon acquiesced to Amy's demands, diffusing the conflict. This instance underscored the efficacy of trust protector powers – an often straightforward and powerful tool for resolving disputes, preventing unnecessary legal expenses, and upholding the trust's integrity. Properly wielded, these powers can significantly influence the smooth operation and preservation of a trust and avoid costly litigation between the trustee and beneficiaries.

Trust Protectors Role

The role of a trust protector, a concept originating from American offshore trusts, is to oversee or moderate the actions of the trustee. Initially, trust protectors were introduced to address concerns about trust companies in smaller countries having unchecked control over assets. Now, trust protectors have become a standard feature in most trusts crafted by attorneys.

The primary function of a trust protector is to act as an independent third party, stepping in during specific unforeseen events, such as the death of the settlor or the establishment of an irrevocable trust. One key responsibility often assigned to trust protectors is the authority to establish a supplemental needs trust for a beneficiary who becomes disabled. This authority is crucial as it prevents the possibility of trust assets inadvertently becoming government property due to a trustee's failure to establish such a trust.

Additionally, a trust protector provides a vital safeguard against trustees who may deviate from the trust's stipulations. They have the power to remove a non-compliant trustee and appoint a successor, circumventing the need for court intervention. In the event of legal disputes, a trust protector also has the discretion to change the jurisdiction of the lawsuit to better protect the interests of the trust. This added layer of oversight ensures that the trust's objectives are upheld and the beneficiaries' interests are safeguarded.

The following is a list of powers commonly granted to a trust protector:

1. The power to modify or amend the administrative and technical provisions of the trust agreement (i) to achieve favorable tax status, (ii) to respond to changes in the code, state law, or the rulings and regulations thereunder, or (iii) to amend the trust agreement to ensure that the settlor's intentions and desires are carried out;

2. The power to remove any trustee of a trust created under the trust agreement;

3. The power to designate the laws of another jurisdiction as the controlling law with respect to the construction, validity, and administration of a particular trust if either (i) the trustee resides in, or administers the trust in, this designated jurisdiction (or in the case of a corporate Trustee, if such corporate Trustee is chartered in this designated jurisdiction) or (ii) the primary beneficiary of the trust resides in this designated jurisdiction, in which event the laws of this designated jurisdiction shall apply to the trust as of the date of the new designation;

4. The power to modify or amend the purposes for which the income and principal of a trust may be distributed, as well as the factors the trustee may consider in making such distributions;

5. The power to change the termination date of a trust created under the trust agreement, either by shortening or lengthening the term thereof, except that the term chosen shall not violate other provisions in the trust agreement regarding the maximum duration of trusts;

6. The power to direct the trustee to distribute or not to distribute trust income or principal to the beneficiary of the trust, as long as such distribution or such withholding of a distribution is within the discretionary powers granted to this trustee, in which case, the trustee shall not be responsible for reviewing, approving, or disapproving any such direction to distribute or not to distribute trust property;

7. The power to direct the trustee to invest or not to invest all or a portion of the property of a trust created under the trust agreement in a particular type or kind of investment;

8. The power to correct ambiguities, including typographical errors, that might otherwise require court reformation or construction;

9. The power to convert any trust created under the trust agreement to a purely discretionary supplemental needs trust, designed to preserve the public benefits eligibility of the primary beneficiary of the trust, the terms and provisions of which shall be determined by the trust protector; and

10. The power to irrevocably release, renounce, suspend, or limit any or all of the powers conferred.

The role of a trust protector is pivotal in enhancing and safeguarding your trust. An attorney is an excellent choice for this position. State laws strictly prohibit attorneys from being beneficiaries of estate planning documents they have prepared for clients. This legal constraint ensures that an attorney, when appointed as a trust protector, cannot gain any beneficial interest in the trust's property. Therefore, an attorney can be entrusted with significant powers to manage and protect your trust interests, without the potential conflicts of interest that might arise with other trust protectors. This arrangement provides a layer of security and integrity to the administration of your trust.

The Trust Protector is Like a Judge

The role of a trust protector is akin to that of a judge, serving as a crucial intermediary in trust administration. In my capacity as a trust protector for numerous trusts, I've rarely needed to exercise this power. Typically, its necessity surfaces during disputes between beneficiaries and trustees. My mere indication of readiness to use trust protector authority has often sufficed to resolve these issues, highlighting its effectiveness in avoiding lengthy legal procedures.

One particularly instructive case in my practice involved a trust I had drafted without trust protector provisions. This omission led to a prolonged three-year legal dispute, incurring over $100,000 in legal fees. This experience underscored the importance of including trust protector powers in trust documents to facilitate more efficient and cost-effective resolution of conflicts, thereby preserving the trust's assets and the beneficiaries' interests.

21: Qualified Income Trusts and Irrevocable Trust for Long-Term Care

There are two specific types of trusts often used in Medicaid long-term care planning: the Qualified Income Trust (QIT) and the Irrevocable Trust. These trusts are designed to protect your estate in the event you require nursing home care. It's a sobering fact that approximately 42% of Americans face severe financial constraints at the end of their lives, with 19% passing away with no financial assets at all. Many clients find themselves unexpectedly needing nursing home care, which can be financially challenging. Typically, long-term care options fall into three categories: personally financed, third-party-financed, and government-based assistance.

To be eligible for government-based assistance for nursing home care or waiver programs, you must satisfy three criteria: a medical necessity for the care, income below a certain threshold, and total assets valued under the limit set by Medicaid rules.

The benefits of qualifying for Medicaid long-term care assistance include:

1. Reduced Costs: Medicaid beneficiaries typically pay about 15% to 20% less than private-pay patients for most services.

2. Prescription Medication Coverage: If you are eligible for a Medicaid program, like nursing home Medicaid or the Community Based Alternatives program, this also qualifies you for a Medicare Part D plan that covers prescription medications and waives all premiums.

3. Deferred Repayment: It could be several years before your surviving family members are required to repay Medicaid, and this kind of 'loan' does not accrue interest.

4. Potential Estate Recovery Avoidance: If your beneficiaries have taken appropriate measures, your estate might evade estate recovery, thus reducing the overall cost of care for the decedent.

It's important to consider these trusts as part of a comprehensive long-term care strategy, especially given the unpredictable nature of future health care needs.

Qualified Income Trusts and Medicaid Eligibility

A Qualified Income Trust (QIT) can be an essential tool in qualifying for Medicaid benefits, especially when personal income exceeds the eligibility threshold. As of January 1, 2024, an individual's income exceeding $2,829 a month would disqualify them from Medicaid. However, considering that nursing home care costs considerably exceed this amount, Congress, through the 1993 Omnibus Budget Reconciliation Act, allowed for income transfer into a trust to meet Medicaid eligibility.

It's important to note that trust and Medicaid laws vary by state. In Texas and twelve other states, there's an income cap for Medicaid. Therefore, what applies in Texas might not be relevant in other states.

Regarding QIT applicability, it's specific to Medicaid nursing home care programs or those directly affected by the Omnibus Budget Reconciliation Act. It does not extend to other programs, such as Community Care, which fall under Title XX of the Social Security Act.

A QIT is funded by all available income, including social security, pensions, and other regular income sources. Any accumulated income in the trust is, upon the death of the individual, reimbursed to the Texas Health and Human Services Commission as a payback to the Texas Medicaid Program.

Transferring assets to qualify for Medicaid is often misunderstood. While it's not illegal to transfer assets for Medicaid long-term care eligibility, such transfers can attract penalties if not done at fair market value. This penalty is in place to prevent last-minute asset transfers before entering a care facility.

Bankruptcy laws and Medicaid have different implications for asset transfers. Bankruptcy has a 5-year look-back for fraudulent transfers, distinct from Medicaid's gifting rules. Additionally, federal gift tax rules, allowing transfers up to $18,000 per year without IRS reporting, should not be confused with Medicaid's reporting requirements for any gifted amount.

Regarding Medicaid eligibility, any transferred assets below fair market value can lead to ineligibility. The ineligibility period is calculated at one day per every $242.13 given away, applicable only during the 60-month look-back period preceding the Medicaid application. The ineligibility period commences once you're in a nursing home and meet all other Medicaid requirements.

It's crucial to understand that gifting with the intent to qualify for Medicaid is not advisable. For those requiring long-term care soon, a gifting strategy is generally inadvisable. However, gifts under $200 within a calendar month are typically excluded from the transfer penalty.

Navigating Irrevocable 5-Year Trusts for Medicaid Planning

In the realm of Medicaid planning, the variety of trusts available can sometimes be overwhelming for clients. It's crucial to differentiate between a Qualified Income Trust (QIT) and an irrevocable 5-year trust, as they serve distinct purposes. A QIT is tailored to manage the income of a Medicaid client, while an irrevocable 5-year trust is designed to handle the assets of a Medicaid client.

The irrevocable 5-year trust is a strategy for those who wish to gift their property to their children, with the intent to wait out the Medicaid 60-month look-back period before applying for benefits. However, several risks are associated with direct gifting. The recipient of the gift might pass away, potentially diverting your assets to unintended parties. There's also the risk of your assets being claimed by a spendthrift spouse of the recipient, creditors in case of the recipient's debt, or the IRS for back-taxes.

Additionally, the recipient might urgently use the funds, or changes in gifting laws could impact your planning.

To mitigate these risks, it's advisable to consider placing your assets into an irrevocable trust that spans at least five years, rather than directly gifting them to family members. This approach provides a safeguarded inheritance for your loved ones while aligning with the requirements to eventually qualify for government assistance through Medicaid. This method offers a more controlled and secure way to manage your assets in the context of Medicaid planning.

22: Epilogue: After Getting a Living Trust

This book aims to illuminate the advantages of establishing a living trust and dispelling the idea that wills are like trust. While it's true that a living trust may not suit everyone, it offers numerous benefits that can apply to many people. I encourage you to thoughtfully consider if a living trust could be the right choice for protecting the interests of your family, loved ones, or even pets.

If you decide to proceed with a living trust, it's imperative to have it drafted by a qualified attorney. The complexities and nuances in creating a living trust are numerous, and the risks of errors are significant. To illustrate, I recently encountered a scenario where a living trust, created online and holding real estate, was brought to my attention. Upon reviewing it, it became evident that the document was so flawed that it left the beneficiaries in a legal quagmire, likely requiring litigation to resolve who the rightful beneficiaries were. This example underscores the importance of professional legal guidance in drafting a living trust, ensuring clarity, legal soundness, and the safeguarding of your intentions.

Ensuring Assets Are Included in Your Living Trust

When clients leave my office with a living trust, I often ask, "How will you ensure that your future assets are included in this trust after your passing?" A primary objective of a living trust is to bypass probate, and this is achievable only when your assets are properly placed within the trust. It's important to note that while certain investments like annuities or retirement accounts can't be directly placed into a revocable trust, aligning their beneficiary designations with the trust can still ensure they benefit from it.

To effectively transfer various assets into the trust, different methods are used based on the asset type:

1. Real estate requires a deed, drafted by an attorney licensed in the relevant state.
2. Bank accounts can be transferred by either renaming the account in the trust's name or designating the trust as a beneficiary.
3. Vehicle ownership is shifted by transferring the title's name.
4. Titled artwork is moved into the trust by updating the title.
5. Household personal effects are assigned through a specific assignment document or listed in an exhibit within the trust.
6. Safe deposit boxes are transferred similarly to bank accounts, either through a name change or beneficiary designation.
7. Stock certificates should be reissued in the trust's name.
8. For a partnership or LLC interest, assignment documents are required, along with modifications to corporate records.
9. Mineral interests necessitate a deed for transfer, while division orders require a separate assignment, often handled by an oil and gas attorney.
10. Promissory notes payable directly to the settlors should be endorsed or assigned to the trust, and the payer should be notified of this change.
11. Savings Bonds can be transferred using the form available at www.treasurydirect.gov/forms/sav1851.pdf.

Each type of asset requires a specific process for inclusion in the trust to ensure smooth transition and management upon the settlor's passing.

Understanding Living Trusts: Titling, Taxation, and Property Transfers

When it comes to titling assets in a living trust, there are several acceptable formats, but they all serve the same fundamental purpose – to clearly identify the trust. Popular formats include:

- "[NAME OF TRUSTEES], Co-Trustees of the [NAME OF TRUST]"
- "[NAME OF TRUSTEES], Co-Trustees of the [NAME OF TRUST]", under Trust Agreement dated [DATE TRUST CREATED], and as may be amended"

If your living trust was drafted by an attorney, you likely received a certificate of trust. This document is a condensed version of your trust, designed to maintain privacy while providing essential information to entities like government agencies, title companies, or financial institutions. If the certificate of trust isn't sufficient for these entities, you may need to provide more detailed information. Should you prefer not to disclose the full trust, consult with your attorney to create a revised certificate that includes the necessary details.

For income tax purposes, a living trust is typically treated as a pass-through entity. This means all income and expenses are reported on your personal tax returns, using your Social Security number instead of a separate tax ID number. However, upon your passing, the trustee will need to obtain a new tax ID number for the trust.

When transferring property into a trust, it's essential to update your insurance policies to cover the trust and its assets. This is especially important for real estate and other significant assets included in the trust.

Regarding vehicles, my general advice is not to transfer them into the trust. This is due to the simplicity of transferring vehicle ownership in Texas without probate, using heirship affidavits or alternative methods. Texas law offers two options for non-probate transfer of vehicles:

1. Establishing joint tenancy with right of survivorship, using the Texas Department of Motor Vehicles form VTR-122.

2. Designating a beneficiary for the vehicle with the Texas Department of Motor Vehicles form VTR-121.

Both of these methods require filing the appropriate forms with the Texas DMV to be effective. This approach simplifies the process and avoids the complexities of including vehicles in a trust, though your attorney may have different recommendations based on specific circumstances and state laws.

Effective Trust Maintenance

Maintaining a trust efficiently involves focusing on two key tasks. Firstly, ensure that all real estate holdings are properly conveyed to the trust. This can be done either immediately or stipulated to occur upon your death. The important part is that the property's title explicitly reflects the trust's ownership.

Secondly, it's crucial to update the beneficiary designations on all your financial accounts to reflect your trust. This includes retirement accounts like IRAs and 401ks, life insurance policies, annuities, and your regular banking accounts such as checking and savings. For most individuals, these two categories - real estate and financial accounts - cover the majority of their assets.

It's worth noting that even if the beneficiary designations are overlooked during your lifetime, a well-crafted estate plan typically includes a safety net, known as a pour-over will. This legal document ensures any remaining personal assets are transferred into your trust upon your death, thereby aligning with your overall estate planning goals.

In essence, good estate planning is not just about setting up a trust; it's also about consistently ensuring that all relevant assets are properly aligned with the trust structure. This proactive approach, combined with a pour-over will as a contingency plan, ensures a comprehensive and effective estate management strategy.

Changing the Beneficiary to the Trust

Changing the beneficiary on your checking, savings, or investment accounts is a crucial step in estate planning and asset management. This ensures that upon your passing, your assets are distributed in accordance with your wishes. The process involves several important steps:

1. Gather Necessary Information: Before initiating changes, ensure you have all required details handy. This includes your account numbers, the

new beneficiary's full name, address, Social Security Number, and date of birth, along with your identification documents for identity verification purposes.

2. Complete the Required Forms or Online Registration: Financial institutions typically require a beneficiary designation form or an online registration process. Accuracy in completing these forms is paramount to prevent future complications.

Specific Procedures for Major Banks:

Chase Bank: Utilize the Transfer on Death Agreement. After filling out the agreement and having it notarized, submit it to Chase via fax at 800-805-3909 or follow the email instructions provided on their platform.

Wells Fargo: Complete the Transfer on Death Application and Agreement, also known as the Transfer on Death Kit. This document must be notarized and then sent to Wells Fargo, with fax options available at 1-844-879-1439.

Bank of America: Account owners can change or add Payable on Death (POD) beneficiaries through Online Banking. Navigate to your account, select "Manage" next to Beneficiaries in the Features menu or on the Information & Services tab. For those without online access, assistance is available at 800.432.1000.

U.S. Bancorp: Contact a banker directly to discuss beneficiary changes, providing the last four digits of each account number involved.

Goldman Sachs: The Transfer on Death (TOD) Beneficiary Form requires a signature from an SVP or a medallion guarantee. For help, contact a representative at 1-800-526-7384.

Capital One Financial: Change your beneficiary online via capitalone.com or by completing a Payable on Death (POD) beneficiary form, requiring notarization and submission through fax or standard mail.

TD Ameritrade: Beneficiary changes can be made online through the account settings, with a Transfer on Death (TOD) Beneficiary Agreement available for completion without the need for notarization.

For Financial Institutions Not Providing Forms Online

Charles Schwab: Offers a step-by-step video guide on beneficiary changes.

Truist Financial, PNC Financial Services, and Edward Jones: Require visiting a branch or contacting your advisor directly, with Edward Jones noting a fee for asset transfers under their Transfer on Death Agreement.

Remember, accounts like IRAs may have specific rules for beneficiary designations. If your estate planning needs are complex or involve a trust, consulting an estate planning attorney is advisable to ensure your beneficiary designations align with your overall estate plan. While bank personnel can assist in the beneficiary change process, they cannot provide legal advice. For questions affecting your estate plan, seeking guidance from an estate planning attorney ensures your decisions are well-informed and aligned with your estate planning objectives.